VOTES FOR WOMEN!

The Fight for Women's Suffrage

VOTES FOR WOMEN!

The Fight for Women's Suffrage

ROSEN
PUBLISHING

Larry A. Van Meter

Published in 2021 by The Rosen Publishing Group, Inc.
29 East 21st Street, New York, NY 10010

Library of Congress Cataloging-in-Publication Data

Names: Van Meter, Larry A., author.
Title: Votes for women! : the fight for women's suffrage / Larry A. Van Meter.
Description: New York : Rosen Publishing, 2021 | Series: Movements and moments that changed America | Audience: Grades: 6-12. | Includes bibliographical references and index.
Identifiers: LCCN 2019018316 | ISBN 9781725342217 (library bound) | ISBN 9781725342200 (pbk.)
Subjects: LCSH: Women--Suffrage--United States--History--Juvenile literature.
Classification: LCC JK1898 .V36 2021 | DDC 324.6/230973--dc23
LC record available at https://lccn.loc.gov/2019018316

Portions of this book originally appeared in *Women Win the Vote: The Hard-Fought Battle for Women's Suffrage.*

Photo Credits: Cover, pp. 3, 40 De Agostini Picture Library/Getty Images; p. 7 Historical Picture Archive/Corbis Historical/Getty Images; pp. 8-9 Everett Historical/Shutterstock.com; p. 13 Gado Images/Alamy Stock Photo; p. 15 Library Of Congress/Wikimedia Commons/File:Esther Morris cph.3a02555.jpg/Public Domain Mark; pp. 21, 30 Stock Montage/Archive Photos/Getty Images; p. 22-23 englishare.net/Wikimedia Commons/File:Marie de France 2.tif/Public Domain Mark; p. 24 PhotoRoman/Shutterstock.com; p. 27 Culture Club/Hulton Archive/Getty Images; pp. 34-35 Print Collector/Hulton Archive/Getty Images; p. 36 Heritage Images/Hulton Fine Art Collection/Getty Images; pp. 44-45 WAVE: The Museums, Galleries and Archives of Wolverhampton/Hulton Fine Art Collection/Getty Images; p. 47 Archive Photos/Getty Images; pp. 49, 53, 58, 68, 82, 85, 90, 96, 97, 103, 105, 108-109 Library of Congress Prints and Photographs Division; p. 65 Private Collection/Wood Ronsaville Harlin, Inc. USA/Bridgeman Images; p. 73 Universal History Archive/Universal Images Group/Getty Images; pp. 78-79 Authenticated News/Archive Photos/Getty Images; p. 101 Ken Florey Suffrage Collection/Gado/Archive Photos/Getty Images; p. 114 Scott Olson/Getty Images; cover and interior pages banner graphic stockish/Shutterstock.com.

CPSIA Compliance Information: Batch #BSR20. For further information contact Rosen Publishing, New York, New York at 1-800-237-9932.

Find us on

CONTENTS

INTRODUCTION

The word "suffrage" means "the right to vote." It comes from the Latin noun *suffragium*, meaning both a vote and the stone or wood tablet on which a vote was cast in the ancient world.

For most of human history, governmental power was exercised by ruling families, or monarchies: a king ruled his country, and his heir (most often his oldest son) would rule after he retired or died. But families are small: how is an individal going to rule an entire country if there are only so many family members to go around? The answer is to make friends with other families and grant them powers as well. In ancient Rome, which exerted a strong influence on the rise of global democracy (government by the people), these ruling families were called the *nobilitas*, the ruling classes. Words such as "class," "rank," "aristocracy," and "nobility" descend from this term. Governmental power lay in the hands of these wealthy families, and their children inherited that power.

In 510 BCE, the Roman nobilitas had gained enough power to overthrow the king, Tarquinius Superbus, who was

Rome had one of the first democratic governments. Male citizens could vote, regardless of their station in life. However, women were not involved.

It wasn't until the 1900s that women were allowed to vote in the United States. Prior to that, women protested and demonstrated in the streets for the right.

an evil, brutal despot, and they instituted a republic, a government by representatives instead of a single monarch. But like the kings before them, members of the nobilitas kept their power within their own families. In ancient Rome, if someone was not in the nobilitas, that person was a plebeian (meaning commoner or working class) and didn't get a say in government—or in most anywhere else either.

At first, only those within the ranks of the nobilitas held political power, but over time, plebeians, who were the soldiers fighting in the nobilitas's many wars and the laborers doing all the nobilitas's work, earned political positions. In 367 CE, the Licinian Laws were passed, which eliminated the distinction between members of the nobilitas and plebeians—they were now equal in the eyes of the law. A "pleb" could now cast a suffragium alongside his "noble" neighbor.

However, although the rise of the plebeians and the passing of the Licinian Laws were major steps forward in the history of democracy, those developments still didn't apply to half the population: women. As a woman, it didn't matter if she were nobilitas or plebeian: suffrage was reserved for men only. And that fact wouldn't change for more than two thousand years.

Many young people in the twenty-first century have grown up in a United States where everybody has the same rights, regardless of their gender, race, or religion. But it hasn't always been that way. The reality is that it's only been that way for a relatively short time, especially regarding suffrage.

The history of how women gained the right to vote is a story of courage and heartbreak, fearlessness and betrayal, hope and frustration, and wisdom and cruelty. Ultimately, though, it is a story of victory.

THE WYOMING EXPERIMENT

In 1869, American women did not have the right to vote. That fact wasn't controversial because no woman anywhere in the world had the right to vote in 1869. But that year, two events occurred that would prove to be important in the struggle for women's voting rights.

The first was that in Washington, DC, the nation's capital, a new constitutional amendment, the Fifteenth Amendment, was being introduced to grant suffrage to African American men. It was an important step in healing the wounds of the Civil War, which had ended four years earlier, and in overcoming the racism that had marked American history. And women's rights activists, who had for many years worked tirelessly to gain the right to vote, were hoping to add women's suffrage to the new law.

The second event was Wyoming's desire for statehood.

The Fifteenth Amendment was ratified, granting African American men the right to vote. This was a victory— but only a partial victory. Unfortunately, women's rights advocates were unsuccessful in adding women's suffrage to the amendment.

However, unlike the ratification of the Fifteenth Amendment, Wyoming's desire for statehood would initiate a chain reaction that ultimately resulted in women's suffrage.

At the center of events in Wyoming was Esther Morris, a saloon owner in South Pass City, one of the largest towns in the territory.

In 1869, there were thirty-seven states in the United States. As was true for many areas in the American West, Wyoming was a "territory," a geographic area that did not yet have statehood status. Like many people in Wyoming, Morris wanted Wyoming to become a state. She had been working with many others to organize a legislature, a governing body that makes laws, for the Wyoming Territory. The Wyoming territorial elections were to take place on September 3, 1869. Those elections were going to be a very important step in Wyoming's bid to become a new state.

The United States was quickly growing. The nation had recently reunified after the Civil War had ended in 1865. Statehood was the goal of all territories. It meant full partnership in this vast, new country. Gaining statehood, however, was difficult. The territories had to prove themselves worthy of entry into the union. In 1869, the population of Wyoming was a meager 8,014, too small to be considered for statehood.[1] The requirement for statehood was a population of more than twenty-five thousand.

Esther Morris had a plan to gain the attention of the lawmakers in the nation's capital.

Esther Morris Goes West

Born in Oswego, New York, in 1814, Esther Hobart McQuigg grew up in an orphanage. Trained to be a

The United States in 1873

This map shows how the United States looked in 1873. At that time, some areas that are part of the modern-day United States, including Wyoming, were not yet states, but were still part of the country as territories.

seamstress as a young girl, she was hardworking and—unlike many women in the nineteenth century—financially successful. At the age of twenty-eight, she married Artemus Slack, a civil engineer. In 1842, they had a son, Archibald. Tragedy struck in 1845 when Artemus died. Esther then moved with Archibald from New York to Illinois to settle Slack's financial affairs. At that time, however, women had few legal rights. Legally, a woman was considered chattel, that is, her husband's property. If the husband died before his wife, she faced a difficult legal battle to gain the family property and money. Esther was unable to secure the Illinois property that her husband had left to her. The harsh legal battles regarding Slack's property left Esther frustrated, making her sensitive to women's rights.[2]

Those legal hardships would play a strong role in forming Esther's inner strength. While in Illinois, she married a local merchant, John Morris. After the birth of twins, Robert and Edward, the Morrises, like thousands of Americans at the time, went west to seek their fortune. In 1868, they moved to South Pass City in the Wyoming Territory, one of the many gold mining towns that were sprouting in the American West.

The Morrises opened a saloon, a successful business that established the couple as influential, well-respected citizens. And like many citizens on the American frontier, the couple wanted statehood for Wyoming.

Esther Morris's Suffrage Strategy

In the same way that states established their own legislatures, the territories also organized legislatures. But a territorial legislature was not only a lawmaking body, it was also required for statehood. If a territory could

Esther Morris's hard work enabled the Wyoming Territory to allow women to vote. This drew people to the area and started a trend across America that resulted in all women in the country getting to vote.

The Equality State

Because it was the first place to grant women the right to vote, Wyoming, the forty-fourth of the United States of America, is known as "the Equality State." It is the tenth-largest state in size, slightly smaller than Oregon and slighter larger than Michigan. At more than 97,000 square miles (251,229 sq km), it is roughly the same size as Iceland or South Korea. Though it is a large state in terms of land area, it is the smallest state in terms of population: in 2019, it had 573,000 people, roughly half the population of the smallest state, Rhode Island, which has about one-sixteenth the land area of Wyoming. The name "Wyoming" is derived from the Munsee Indian word *xwemamenk*, meaning "at the big river flat."

run a government, it would prove that it could handle the responsibility of statehood. Two candidates for the territorial legislature, William H. Bright and Herman G. Nickerson, were in South Pass City for the elections. Bright was the Democratic Party candidate for the legislature, and Nickerson was a Republican candidate. Both Bright and Nickerson were veterans of the Civil War, and both were acquaintances of Esther Morris's. They both held Morris in high regard. Because Morris was one of the most prominent citizens in South Pass City, Bright and Nickerson knew that gaining her approval would help to secure election to the legislative office.

Morris was admired for her fairness, honesty, and confidence. She commanded respect from everyone she met. Morris realized that the best strategy to earn statehood for Wyoming was to bring thousands of people to live there. Her idea to get them there was to give women the right to vote. As the elections neared, Morris approached Bright and Nickerson with her idea. At first, they were stunned. But both men quickly recognized the importance of Morris's suggestion. Even those people who had never heard of the Wyoming Territory would take notice if Wyoming was considering women's suffrage. Perhaps when people learned about Wyoming, they would want to move there.

Bright was the first to promise Morris that, if elected to the legislature, he would introduce a women's suffrage bill. Not wanting to be outdone by his opponent, Nickerson also promised that he would introduce such a bill if elected.

Bright won the election. Would he be true to his word? It was one thing to promise suffrage to a woman before the elections but quite another to introduce a women's suffrage bill in the legislature. The first Wyoming territorial legislature convened in Cheyenne on October 1, 1869. Bright was elected president of the nine-man Senate.

Esther Morris's Strategy Gains Momentum

On November 9, Bright announced during a Senate session that in a few days, he was going to make a major proposal. Sure enough, on November 12, he stood up and announced his bill: "An Act to Grant the Women of Wyoming Territory the Right of Suffrage and to Hold Office." There were a few laughs and insults thrown at Bright, but the senators had known in advance that the bill was coming.

After the announcement, Bright had two weeks to convince his fellow senators to vote for the bill. None of the other senators really believed that women should have the right to vote. But they did understand that the bill was a big deal. Bright tried to convince the senators that, whether or not they actually agreed with the bill, passage of the bill would be a dramatic and symbolic statement for the Wyoming Territory. Furthermore, passage of the bill could draw homesteaders out to the new territory, maybe enough to qualify for statehood.

Bright, working with his wife, Julia, and Esther Morris, managed to be very persuasive. The suffrage bill passed by a six to two margin. (One senator was absent.) This was the first time in history that a women's suffrage bill had passed in a legislative body. But Bright's "Female Suffrage Act," as it would become known in the territory, was only one-third of the way to becoming law. After its passage in the territory's Senate, it would go to the territory's House of Representatives for approval. If it was approved there, the territory's governor, John Campbell, would then have to approve and sign it.

Esther Morris and Julia Bright, thrilled by the bill's success passing that first test, began a letter-writing campaign to the territorial representatives, urging them to pass the women's suffrage bill. Even more important, the two major newspapers in Cheyenne endorsed the bill. The *Wyoming Tribune*, for example, announced that the bill "is likely to be THE measure of the session, and we are glad our Legislature has taken the initiative in this movement, which [is] destined to become universal. Better to appear to lead than hinder when a movement is inevitable."[3]

Despite the letter-writing and the favorable treatment in the newspapers, there was heated debate on the bill. As in the Senate, there was opposition to the bill in the House. One representative, Ben Sheeks, joked that the minimum age in the bill (eighteen) should be changed to thirty, on the theory that no woman would admit to being thirty years old. Men were convinced that women were not serious about getting involved in American government. Many men—and women as well—believed that women were too emotional and too weak to have a say in politics. Many people feared that women's suffrage would disturb the traditional household arrangements, where husbands and fathers dominated. But after the debates, the eleven-member House voted on the bill. By the narrowest of margins, the House passed the bill: six votes for, four against, with one abstention. The only hurdle remaining was Governor Campbell.

Very few people actually believed that the "Female Suffrage Act" would become Wyoming law. Most of the senators and representatives in Wyoming were members of the Democratic Party. But Governor Campbell was a Republican who constantly found himself at odds with the legislature. That rivalry was one of the reasons that many of the legislators had passed the bill. They fully expected Campbell to veto, or reject, it. In other words, the legislators promised Bright that they would vote for the bill, but they never expected it to become law. They believed that their political rival, Governor Campbell, would never sign it. It was public knowledge that Campbell did not support women's suffrage. And if he were to veto the bill, then its only chance of becoming law would be for the legislature to override his veto. The legislature needed a two-thirds majority to override a governor's veto—and the Wyoming legislators knew no such majority existed. If Campbell vetoed the bill, it would "die"—it would not become law.

But by the time the women's suffrage bill landed on his desk, Governor Campbell had experienced a change of heart. He had noticed the impassioned defense of the bill by some men and women in the territory and the favorable treatment of the bill in the state newspapers. He understood that passage of the women's suffrage bill would not only be an important moment in Wyoming history but also in American history. So on December 10, 1869, Governor Campbell signed the women's suffrage bill into law.

"On Behalf of the Women of Wyoming"

For the first time, women had the right to vote. Of course, that right was limited to women in the Wyoming Territory, and there was no guarantee that Wyoming would keep women's suffrage if it became a state. Nevertheless, for at least as long as Wyoming was a territory, women could vote.

But Esther Morris's work as a feminist pioneer was not over. Just a few months after women's suffrage was legalized in Wyoming, Morris became a judge in South Pass City. She was the first woman to hold a judicial position.[4] On February 17, 1870, Morris was granted a commission to serve as justice of the peace for South Pass City, a position she held for eight months.

Wyoming gained statehood in 1890, becoming the forty-fourth state in the Union. To the delight of women's suffrage activists all over America, Wyoming elected to keep women's suffrage when it became an official state. Statehood was celebrated in Cheyenne, the capital city, on July 24, 1890.

This illustration shows women in Cheyenne, Wyoming, voting in 1888. Wyoming was the first place in the United States that allowed women to vote and to hold political office.

Marie de France

For most of human history, women were prevented from learning how to read and write. And even those few who were educated did not publish their works. An early exception was Marie de France (ca. 1140–ca. 1200), who was born in France but moved to England, likely as a young girl. Scholars believe that she was a noblewoman—perhaps even the half-sister of the English king Henry II, who was also born in France. Marie wrote a series of popular love poems (*lais*) in the second half of the twelfth century. One of the poems, *Lanval*, is about a knight in King Arthur's court, Lanval, who is falsely accused of insulting King Arthur's wife. Lanval's true love, a fairy queen, convinces Arthur that the charges against Lanval are false. It is one of the earliest stories where the testimony of a woman is valued. Marie's lais would exert a strong influence on the chivalric, romantic literature of the Middle Ages and Renaissance.

Marie de France was a rare female writer and noblewoman living in the twelfth century.

The Wyoming state flag was born during a time of change in the United States, when women were gaining more rights, starting in Wyoming itself.

The honor of presenting the new state flag to the governor fell to Morris, then in her seventies, who said:

> On behalf of the women of Wyoming, and in grateful recognition of the high privilege of citizenship that has been conferred upon us, I have the honor to present to the state of Wyoming this beautiful flag. May it always remain the emblem of our liberties, "and the flag of the union forever."[5]

To present the newest flag in the United States to the governor was a great honor, but it was also a fitting tribute to Esther Morris, who, after all, had been one of the pioneers in the women's suffrage movement.

THE UNITED STATES: THE BIRTHPLACE OF WOMEN'S SUFFRAGE

The year of Wyoming's revolutionary suffrage bill, 1869, is an important date in the fight for women's voting rights. But the struggle for enfranchisement (another term for the right to vote) had raged for several decades before then. As a matter of fact, by 1869, many women's suffrage activists, such as Elizabeth Cady Stanton, Susan B. Anthony, and Lucy Stone, had become household names in America. They had become famous, both as voting rights activists and antislavery activists, and though they had seen the end of slavery, they had not yet achieved voting rights for women. Women's suffrage had come to Wyoming, but women were denied that right everywhere else in the United States. Americans, however, weren't alone in that fact: no women anywhere else in the world had the right to vote, either.

The fight for women's suffrage had come a long way. But the seeds of women's suffrage had been planted almost a century before the success in Wyoming.

Christine de Pisan

Born in Italy, Christine de Pisan (ca. 1364–1430) grew up in France because her father, Tommaso di Benvenuto da Pizzano, was the court astrologer for the French king. Tommaso, recognizing his daughter's curiosity and intelligence, permitted her an education, a rarity at that time. Widowed at age twenty-five, she began to earn her living as a writer, the first woman in recorded history to do so. In 1405, she wrote *The Book of the City of Ladies*, which argued against the traditional belief that women were naturally immoral, frivolous, and hysterical. Still widely read today, *The Book of the City of Ladies* is a rigorous defense of women's intelligence and dignity, and it presently stands as one of the foundational works in the struggle for women's rights.

The Birth of the Women's Suffrage Movement

Women's suffrage is just one of many issues that make up women's rights. For most of history, women did not have the same legal status as men. In most cultures, women were considered men's property, and they had very little control over their own lives. So few were educated and so few had any measure of freedom that there is almost no record of what they actually wanted. Women were at the mercy of men, who had complete control of not only women's lives but also most forms of media.

Christine de Pisan was the first woman to make a living from writing.

It's a mistake to believe that the fight for women's rights is a relatively new development. It seems natural they would have wanted equal rights, but because they had so little access to media, there's very little record of this want or any fight for it.

In 1789, the United States and France would play roles in the drama of women's suffrage. Two other years in American history are more famous—1776 (the signing of the Declaration of Independence) and 1787 (the drafting of the US Constitution). But 1789 is noteworthy because that year, the new United States ratified its Constitution, the document that defined the American government.

Between the years 1776 and 1789, a debate about voting rights raged among the Founding Fathers of the United States. All of them agreed that the right to vote was very important. But *who* should have the right to vote? In the Declaration of Independence, Thomas Jefferson wrote these profound words: "We hold these truths to be self-evident: that all men are created equal." Those were bold and revolutionary words, implying that all men—regardless of where they were born or who their parents were—should have the chance at freedom and liberty. Though these were true and hopeful words in 1776, they excluded more than half the American population. Women were not considered equal, and they certainly were not considered when the Founding Fathers were debating the issue of suffrage. Many of the Founding Fathers were wealthy landowners who thought that only those who owned property should be granted suffrage.

Abigail Adams: "Remember the Ladies"

Just like Jefferson and Benjamin Franklin, John Adams, a lawyer from Massachusetts, was an original member of the Continental Congress. As the Continental Congress met in the summer of 1776 to declare the colonies independent from England, Adams and his colleagues understood that they were building a new country. Though they were all united in their desire to build a country free from tyranny and injustice, many were unsure about how they should organize this new country.

Adams, whose family owned a large farm in eastern Massachusetts, believed that only male property owners should have the right to vote. Indeed, that restriction was the law in all the colonies at the time of the Declaration of Independence. But should it remain the law when the new country broke away from England? Several men in the Continental Congress were calling for an expansion of voting rights to men who did not own property. Adams was shocked at this suggestion, saying:

> [I]t is dangerous to open up so fruitful a source of controversy and altercation as would be opened by attempting to alter the qualifications of voters; there will be no end of it. New claims will rise; women will demand a vote; lads from twelve to twenty-one will think their rights not enough attended to; and every man who has not a farthing will demand an equal voice.[1]

To Adams and many other men, "universal suffrage" (a term meaning that any adult could vote) was a frightening idea. Adams wanted the new American government—a democracy—to be different from the monarchy in England. However, he wanted the suffrage rules to be similar to those in England, where property ownership was the chief requirement for the right to vote.

But Adams's own wife, Abigail, was afraid that the Continental Congress was ignoring too many people's voices, particularly women's voices. In March 1776, she wrote a letter to her husband:

> I long to hear you have declared an independency, and, by the way, in the new code of laws which I suppose it will be necessary for you to make, I

Abigail Adams tried to persuade her husband to consider adding women's rights to the Declaration of Independence, but to no avail. Still, her words would embolden women who came after her demanding equality.

desire you would remember the ladies, and be more generous and favorable to them than your ancestors. Do not put such unlimited power into the hands of husbands.[2]

Later in the same letter, Abigail warned her husband that if he did not include women in the new government, they would "foment a rebellion." These were bold words, especially for the wife of a prominent member of the Continental Congress. John Adams wrote back to his wife: "The Declaration's wording specifies that 'all men are created equal.'"

Abigail's words—"Remember the ladies"—would become a famous rallying cry for women's suffrage, but her husband ignored them.

Thomas Paine and *Common Sense*

Another person who disagreed with John Adams was Thomas Paine. Born in England in 1737, Paine rose to prominence in England as a defender of workers' rights. In 1773, Paine met Benjamin Franklin in London. There is a new spirit of independence in the colonies, Franklin said to Paine. In Europe, every man is subject to the king, but in America, things can be different: every man can decide his own destiny. Persuaded by Franklin, Paine moved to the Massachusetts colony and saw that Franklin was right—there was a greater sense of freedom in this "New World." The American colonists did see themselves as loyal subjects of the English king, George III, but a sense of individual freedom was emerging.

Inspired by the independent spirit in the colonies' rebellion, Paine wrote a pamphlet called *Common Sense*, published in January 1776. It was wildly popular, ultimately becoming the best-selling document in America in the eighteenth century. *Common Sense* passionately argued for American independence from England, but, just as significant, it argued for "large and equal representation" in the new government that would replace the old regime.[3] Paine meant that all citizens should have the right to vote, regardless of their gender and whether or not they were wealthy.

Paine's theories on suffrage were considered radical. The debates about who should have the right to vote became too heated for the authors of the Constitution to handle. Was John Adams right—that only property owners should have suffrage? Or were Abigail Adams and Thomas Paine right—that all citizens should have suffrage?

The authors of the Constitution ultimately decided to do nothing about the issue. In the Constitution approved in 1789, there were no specific laws regarding suffrage. This was not an oversight by the Founding Fathers, but rather a strategy to leave voting rights to each individual state rather than in the hands of the federal government.

Though the US Constitution in its original form in 1789 did not grant universal suffrage, the foundation had been laid by those who had spoken out in support of votes for women.

The Revolution in France

In France, 1789 is known as *L'Année Cruciale*, that is, "The Crucial Year." As the United States had a few years earlier, France was experiencing its own revolution. After centuries of monarchy, the French people seized power and started a democracy. Influenced by the American Declaration of Independence, the French wrote their own document,

The Declaration of the Rights of Man and Citizen. The foundations of the document were the ideas of "liberty, equality, and fraternity." In the new France, everyone was to have an equal chance at a good life. The document consisted of seventeen articles, most of which were about the right of French citizens to govern themselves. The first declaration stated, "Men are born free and remain free and equal in rights."

Heavily influenced by the Founding Fathers in the United States, the French revolutionaries would soon gather to write their own constitution and bring democracy to France. And, as was true in America, the question of women's suffrage became an important topic. The first French constitution, adopted in 1791, was primarily made to ensure that France would never again be ruled by a monarch. Women's suffrage did not seem such an important issue at the time. But French women had fought side-by-side with men during the French Revolution, so they wanted their voices heard in the new French government as well.

One such voice was Olympe de Gouges, one of the first women to argue for women's suffrage in France. Born in 1748, de Gouges was the daughter of a butcher from southwest France. She moved to Paris as a teenager and became a writer. Excited by the possibilities in post-revolution France, de Gouges wrote a pamphlet, *The Declaration of the Rights of Woman and Citizen*, in 1791. Modeled after *The Declaration of the Rights of Man and Citizen*, de Gouges's *Declaration* also consisted of seventeen articles, each one mimicking the famous articles set down in 1789. De Gouges's first declaration was "Woman is born free and is equal to man in rights." Her sixth declaration argued that "[t]he law should be the expression of the

The Women's March on Versailles

One of the reasons that the French Revolution is such an important historical event is that it involved so much direct action by women. The most important of these actions was the Women's March, which occurred on October 5, 1789. On that morning, hundreds of women gathered at the Hotel de Ville in Paris to protest food shortages and the price of bread, which had risen dramatically. Feeling that their voices were not being heard, they decided to march directly to the king's palace, called Versailles, 12 miles (19 km) away. As the women made their way to Versailles, word spread quickly, and soon those hundreds became thousands, and by the time they got to the palace, there were more than six thousand women, many carrying pitchforks, brooms, kitchen knives, torches, and clubs. Upon their arrival, the women demanded to speak to the king, Louis XVI. Terrified at the sight of these angry women, Louis at first refused to meet with them, but he relented, ultimately agreeing to disperse bread to the marchers.

The Women's March in Paris is captured in this painting. The women's determination and formidable numbers made King Louis XVI change his mind about keeping bread from citizens.

Olympe de Gouges advocated for women's rights by writing her own declaration. For her boldness, however, she was executed.

general will. All citizenesses and citizens should take part, in person or by their representatives."[4] This was a bold assertion that implied women should have the right to vote.

De Gouges wrote her declaration during a dangerous time in France, known as the Reign of Terror. Between 1792 and 1794, tens of thousands of French citizens were executed by the guillotines in public spectacles. Because of her writings, de Gouges was labeled a troublemaker and executed by guillotine on November 3, 1793.

Nevertheless, despite the protests of thousands of French women, France's new constitution excluded women from voting. As in America, French women would have a long wait for the right to vote, not receiving suffrage until 1945.

THE PHILOSOPHY OF
WOMEN'S SUFFRAGE

Before the French Revolution, France, like most countries in western civilization, was a monarchy. Believing that they had divine powers, the French kings had, over the centuries, divided the French people into three classes, or "Estates" (the French word is *États*). The First Estate was the church. The Second Estate was the aristocracy, which included the king and his family, and the various aristocratic ranks, such as dukes (*ducs*), earls (*comtes*), and viscounts (*vicomtes*). The Third Estate was everybody else. All the privileges belonged to the First and Second Estates.

The French Revolution ended that system: the revolutionaries eliminated the First and Second Estates, setting the stage for the rise in global democracies. The French Revolution, combined with the American Revolution across the Atlantic Ocean, electrified the world, though perhaps nowhere more so than in England. Many in England were excited by the spirit of freedom in France, excited by the promise of democracy. Due to the involvement of women during the revolution, now it was possible that everyone could help to change a country's government for the better. Though French women were denied the right to vote, the French Revolution, with its motto of "liberty, equality, and fraternity," was still viewed by some people as a sign that better times were on the way for women.

A Vindication of the Rights of Woman

One of the first in England to see how the French Revolution could benefit women was Mary Wollstonecraft. Wollstonecraft was born in London in 1759, the second of six children. By the time Wollstonecraft was a teenager, she knew that she wanted to become a writer. But writing was a difficult profession, especially for women. Most people often saw women as less intelligent than men and were unlikely to read the work of a woman writer. Writing was an especially rough career choice for Mary Wollstonecraft, who had received very little formal schooling. But thanks to a famous public debate she had with England's most influential philosopher, Edmund Burke (1729–1797), Wollstonecraft earned a reputation as one of the great minds in Europe.

Wollstonecraft recognized that despite the democratic potential of the French Revolution, women were still excluded from politics. So in 1792, she began to write her most famous work, A Vindication of the Rights of Woman.

During Wollstonecraft's lifetime, many people believed that men were governed by reason and women were governed by emotion. In A Vindication of the Rights of Woman, Wollstonecraft exposed those notions as prejudices. "I wish," Wollstonecraft wrote, "to persuade women to endeavour to acquire strength, both of mind and body."[1]

To Wollstonecraft, men had "deeply rooted prejudices" against women.[2] Furthermore, argued Wollstonecraft, men

Mary Wollstonecraft was a powerful, persuasive writer who challenged great philosophical men of her time, such as Edmund Burke.

had invented those prejudices and used them to exclude women from government. Wollstonecraft believed that if women received the same education as men, then men and women could be equal partners in society.

Wollstonecraft's most radical suggestion in *A Vindication of the Rights of Woman*, however, was that women should have a voice in government. In Chapter IX of *Vindication*,

A Vindication of the Rights of Men

Not everyone was on the side of the French revolutionaries. Edmund Burke, a well-known English writer and philosopher, wrote a pamphlet called *Reflections on the Revolution in France* in 1790. He contended that people who were not members of the upper class should know their place and stay out of government. Though *Reflections* was popular, many writers defended the French Revolution. One of the most important defenses was *A Vindication of the Rights of Men*, written by Mary Wollstonecraft in 1790. *Vindication* was a best seller and made her an overnight sensation. She had the courage to argue with the most famous philosopher of the time. Her argument also was more reasoned, forceful, and compassionate than Burke's. While Burke argued that aristocratic privileges were "natural" rights, Wollstonecraft argued that all men are born equal, so any rights they have are obtained throughout life rather than granted by God.

she wrote, "Women ought to have representatives, instead of being arbitrarily governed without having any direct share allowed them in the deliberations of government."[3] Wollstonecraft argued both that women should have a say in government and that women should be in government, which were very extreme ideas at the time.

Today, *A Vindication of the Rights of Woman* stands as one of the foundational works in the philosophy of women's rights. Many people during Wollstonecraft's lifetime, however, thought that she was dangerous. As a result, she was subject to a large amount of public abuse. One author, Horace Walpole, called her a "hyena in petticoats," and two books making fun of Wollstonecraft became best sellers: *A Vindication of the Rights of Brutes* and *A Sketch of the Rights of Boys and Girls.*[4]

The abuse in England became so bad for Wollstonecraft that she left the country, spending most of the rest of her life in other European countries. She was known wherever she went, her work having been translated into many languages. She died in 1797, while giving birth to a daughter, Mary. Eventually, the younger Mary would also become a writer. She wrote one of the most famous and influential novels in history, *Frankenstein*, published in 1818.

In the years following Mary Wollstonecraft's death, *A Vindication of the Rights of Woman* would grow in importance for women's rights in general and for women's suffrage specifically. But it would be several decades after Mary Wollstonecraft's death before her pioneering work would bear fruit.

"The Domestic Saint"

John Adams had reminded his wife, Abigail, that the Declaration of Independence asserted only that "all men are created equal." However, there was a growing frustration in the United States with the fact that only men were involved in government. Many women wanted to be involved as well. Women's rights pioneers in Europe had given hope to American women, who now believed that the time was right for them to seek equal rights. In the first half of the nineteenth century, there were several important developments in America that would lay the foundation for women's voting rights.

Perhaps the biggest hurdle that women had to overcome was their traditional role throughout the centuries. At the beginning of the 1800s, women were trapped in a system some historians call "the cult of domesticity." This was a belief that women's lives should be limited to their homes. According to the historian Martha J. Cutter:

> [T]he predominant image for women in the early and middle nineteenth century was the Domestic Saint, an image which focused on women's attributes of piety [religiousness], purity, submissiveness, and domesticity.[5]

In short, "women were to live for others," not for themselves.[6] This belief had widespread popularity in the United States and convinced many people that women should not be active in politics. Politics were reserved for men; women were to stay at home. The woman who submitted to the cult of domesticity was known as a "true woman."

For centuries, women did everything around the house and for their children and husbands. They did not have jobs outside of the home.

In many ways, then, women in the nineteenth century were locked into domestic roles. But thanks to the work of women such as Olympe de Gouges and Mary Wollstonecraft, rumors were spreading that women could excel outside—as well as inside—their homes. But the cult of domesticity was very powerful: many men and women argued that women should not be looking outside the home for fulfillment. A typical book of the 1800s assured women "that the surest pathway to the highest happiness and honor lies through the peaceful domain of wifehood and motherhood ... To the true woman home is her throne."[7] Looking outside that "domain," it was believed, could only lead to trouble. Women who did not practice the "four cardinal virtues" of piety, purity, submissiveness, and domesticity were often punished. It was in this culture that the pioneers of the women's suffrage movement had to work, making their progress very difficult.

The Troy Female Seminary

Not all women were happy with the cult of domesticity. Many American women in the first half of the nineteenth century tried to break out of the roles society forced upon them. One of those women was Emma Hart Willard, who founded the Troy Female Seminary. Born in 1787 near Hartford, Connecticut, Emma Hart was the sixteenth of her father's seventeen children. At that time, American girls were given very little education. Most Americans even believed that girls were incapable of learning difficult subjects, such as geometry. But at age twelve, Emma taught herself geometry.[8] Knowing that other girls could learn difficult subjects, Emma dedicated her life to educating girls.

She began teaching while still a teenager. By age twenty, she was in charge of a boys' and girls' school in Vermont. She married a physician, Dr. John Willard, in 1809. In September 1821, Emma Hart Willard opened the Troy Female Seminary in Troy, New York. Troy Female Seminary was a radical school. There were girls' schools in America at that time, but they were known as "finishing schools." At these schools, teachers trained girls to be virtuous, obedient housewives. Emma Willard wanted her school to be different.

Willard believed that girls' studies should be just as demanding as those of boys. According to historian Elisabeth Griffin:

> Willard was the first educator to replace the traditional offerings of female academies with a rigorous program of instruction. Although she called her school a "female seminary," she in fact aspired to make the classical and scientific curricula of men's colleges available to young women.[9]

In addition to religious and moral education, girls at Troy learned algebra, foreign languages, music, literature,

Emma Hart Willard went beyond the expected for a woman of her times and opened a school that taught women similar subjects to men.

philosophy, art, and psychology. Girls had been traditionally barred from most of those subjects.

Willard, according to biographer John Lord, "was one of the first to demonstrate that there are no subjects which young men can grasp which cannot equally be mastered by young ladies."[10] Willard's educational system became known as the "Troy plan." About two hundred schools modeled on the "Troy plan" opened all over the United States in the nineteenth century. Graduates of Troy Female Seminary founded many of these schools.[11]

The Troy Female Seminary supported Mary Wollstonecraft's belief that women deserved education equal to that of men. Though many Americans believed that "true women" must submit to the cult of domesticity, there were others who believed that true women could do other things, too.

Oberlin College

Another important milestone in the women's rights movement occurred just a few years later, when Oberlin College opened its doors to women. Two missionaries, John J. Shipherd and Philo P. Stewart, founded Oberlin College in northeast Ohio in 1833. They named the college in honor of Jean-Frederic Oberlin, a French missionary and philanthropist whom Shipherd and Stewart greatly admired. Shipherd and Stewart wanted their new college to be a shining light for reform. They knew that there were many things wrong in America: slavery was still legal, and women were trapped in their domestic roles. The two missionaries believed that Oberlin could make a difference and perhaps lead the way in reforming those problems.

In 1835, Oberlin became the first college to admit African American men. Then, in 1837, Oberlin admitted its first women students. Those four women were Mary Kellogg, Mary Caroline Rudd, Mary Hosford, and Elizabeth Prall. All but Kellogg earned their degrees, becoming, in 1841, the first women college graduates in the United States.

A few months after Oberlin began to admit women students, the Mount Holyoke Female Seminary opened on November 8, 1837. Located in South Hadley, Massachusetts, it was the first women's college in America. Like Emma Willard, founder Mary Lyon (1797–1849) believed that women should receive the same education as men. Mount Holyoke used the same textbooks used at men's colleges, especially those for math and science. Wishing to challenge the common prejudice that women could not master the sciences, Lyon required her students to take at least seven courses in math and science in order to graduate. Lyon herself taught chemistry.

Those three revolutionary institutions, Troy Female Seminary (now the Emma Willard School), Oberlin College, and Mount Holyoke College, are still in operation.

Mary Lyon was also a champion of women's education in the 1800s.

For a long time, the cult of domesticity held a powerful grip on American women, convincing them that their duty was in the home—and in the home alone. By the 1840s, however, that grip was loosening. More and more women were seeking opportunities that did not exist before. Soon, more girls' schools based on the "Troy plan" opened, and more colleges admitted women students. More important, those new schools produced women graduates who would become major players in reform movements, chief among them the abolition of slavery and the promotion of women's suffrage.

4

ELIZABETH CADY STANTON AND THE SENECA FALLS CONVENTION

In 1776, when Thomas Jefferson wrote, "We hold these truths to be self evident, that all men are created equal" in the Declaration of Independence, he could not have foreseen just how influential those words would become. But once they had been written, those words would become a rallying cry for many social reforms. Two of the most important social-reform issues in the nineteenth century in the United States were the abolition of slavery and women's suffrage.

If everyone was created equal, then why in America did slavery still exist, and why were women still excluded from suffrage? Soon after the American and French Revolutions, reform societies emerged to deal with the inequality that still continued. In the United States, especially, concerned Americans formed several abolition societies. Some of the most famous were the Society for the Abolition of Slavery, the American Anti-Slavery Society, and the Manumission (a word meaning "to free from slavery") Society. Women were among the most active members of these groups because they saw similarities between their living conditions and those of slaves.

The rise of women's suffrage organizations in the United States was directly linked to the abolitionist movement. It was women's participation in abolition societies (and their newfound educational opportunities at schools such as Troy Seminary) that gave women the experience and confidence to launch the women's suffrage movement in America. So it should be no surprise that many of the pioneers of the women's suffrage movement were themselves prominent abolition activists.

Elizabeth Cady Stanton

One of the most famous of those women's suffrage pioneers was Elizabeth Cady Stanton. The eighth of eleven children, Stanton was born in Johnstown, New York, in 1815, to Daniel and Margaret Cady. Daniel Cady was a successful lawyer who had served one term in the US Congress. He ultimately achieved the position of New York Supreme Court justice. Despite the success of Daniel Cady, the Cady home was often filled with sadness. Five of Elizabeth's brothers and sisters died in early childhood.

Smart, curious, energetic, and wanting to please her father, young Elizabeth wanted to learn everything that she could. Because Elizabeth showed a great deal of intelligence, her father sent her to a private tutor, Simon Hosack, who taught her Greek, mathematics, and chess. Those subjects were usually reserved for boys, but Elizabeth excelled at them. Even after her lessons were over, Elizabeth studied in her father's private library, reading every book she could find. It was in her father's large collection of law books

Elizabeth Cady Stanton was one of the most well-known abolitionists and suffragists in New York.

that Elizabeth first learned about the oppression of slaves and women.

One legal case in particular made a lasting impression on young Elizabeth. One of the Cadys' neighbors, Flora Campbell, had saved up money to buy a farm. After purchasing the farm, she married and soon gave birth to a son. But Campbell's husband died suddenly, and the land was given to the young son, who had no interest in farming. Campbell was frustrated, demanding through the courts that the land be returned to her. She had bought the land herself and believed that she was the rightful landowner. But the court ruled in favor of the son.

Campbell went to Daniel Cady to seek legal advice. She had purchased the property with her own money, so why should ownership of the property go to her son when her husband died? With Elizabeth nearby listening to the conversation, Daniel Cady explained to Campbell that, according to New York law, when a property-owning woman marries, her land immediately becomes her husband's property. Furthermore, if he dies, the property falls into the hands of the nearest male heir. There was nothing anyone could do.

Infuriated, Elizabeth grabbed a knife from the kitchen and ran back to her father's library to cut out the offensive law from the book. Daniel Cady stopped her from cutting the page and gently explained that her actions would not make the law disappear. But memories of this incident remained with Elizabeth for the rest of her life. At that moment, she decided to devote her life to fighting discrimination.

At age fifteen, Elizabeth began attending the Troy Female Seminary. She excelled in her studies, moving toward the top of her class in every subject. Though she would become

Troy's most famous student, she did not finish her studies there. She left during her second year, returning home to a life of leisure.

Most girls, after finishing school, found husbands and settled down to quiet lives of servitude. And, indeed, it seemed as though that would be the path for Elizabeth. She was one of the best students in the history of Troy Female Seminary, but she had no opportunity for higher education. At that time, American women could not go to college (Oberlin College would not allow women until 1837). Frustrated by her lack of opportunity but resigned to her fate, Elizabeth spent the next few years doing the things that eligible young women traditionally did—attending parties, socials, and church. She never lost her love of learning and remained an avid reader for the rest of her life.

Abolition and Suffrage: Partners

Elizabeth Cady's life dramatically changed in 1839 when she started spending more time with her cousin, Gerrit Smith, in Peterboro, New York. He was an intellectual with a powerful, instantly likeable personality. He was also one of the most important abolition activists in America during that time, serving as the president of the New York branch of the American Anti-Slavery Association from 1836 to 1839.

Because of his political career, in which he had to work with people who had a wide range of political beliefs, Daniel Cady had forbidden his family to discuss abolition at home. At the Smith home, however, there was constant talk about the immorality of slavery. The Smith home was one of the centers of abolition activism in America. Many of the prominent abolitionists of the day were frequent houseguests. The atmosphere electrified Elizabeth Cady, who spent more time with the Smiths than at her own home. It was in the Smith home that she vowed to devote her life to the abolitionist cause.

It was also in the Smith home that Cady met a man named Henry Brewster Stanton, who, like Gerrit Smith, was a famous abolitionist. Stanton had gained fame as an antislavery activist in Ohio. In the early 1830s, as a student at Lane Seminary in Cincinnati, Stanton had led a walkout of fifty students who protested the school's anti-abolition policy. These fifty students, known as the "Lane Rebels," transferred to Oberlin College in Ohio. Stanton moved to New York in the late 1830s to work as secretary of the American Anti-Slavery Association.

Elizabeth Cady and Henry Stanton fell in love immediately, and within a month after first meeting, they were engaged. Cady's family was angry. They disapproved of the match on many counts. They felt that the couple had not known each other long enough to marry, and they did not like the fact that Stanton was poor. The Cadys also disapproved of Stanton's abolitionism. They thought that abolitionists were too radical.

Despite this, Cady married Stanton on May 1, 1840. She was twenty-four years old; he was thirty-five. Cady's parents did not attend the wedding, even though the ceremony occurred at their home. Stanton had a magnificent honeymoon planned for his wife. He was taking her to London, England, to attend the first World Anti-Slavery Convention, to be held in June 1840.

Stanton believed that the conference would strengthen his wife's dedication to the abolition cause. The conference, in fact, also spurred her to a deeper involvement in the women's rights movement.

Humiliation in London

When the Stantons arrived in London, they stayed at the same boarding house as many of the women abolitionists. There, Elizabeth Cady Stanton met Lucretia Mott, a famous Quaker preacher. Quakers, also called the Society of Friends, were a group of Christians who supported women's rights and allowed women to serve in leadership positions within their church.

By the time of the World Anti-Slavery Convention in 1840, Lucretia Mott was already a famous American activist. She was intelligent, sensitive, and so well respected that she became a Quaker minister in her Philadelphia church in 1818, at the age of twenty-eight. She was also an active abolitionist. Her home was a station along the Underground Railroad, which helped runaway slaves get to free states and to Canada in the 1800s.

Convinced that women could have a powerful voice in ending slavery, in 1833, Mott founded the world's first women's abolition organization, the Philadelphia Female Anti-Slavery Society. Mott gained recognition as a persuasive public speaker, touring the East Coast and Midwest, arguing for the abolition of slavery.

The World Anti-Slavery Convention opened on June 12, 1840, at the Freemason's Hall on Great Queen Street in London. Thomas Clarkson, an English abolitionist, was named president of the proceedings, and Henry Stanton was named secretary. There were five black delegates at the convention, all of whom were freed slaves: Henry Beckford and Louis Lecesne of Jamaica, Samuel Prescod of Barbados, M. L'Instant of Haiti, and Edward Barratt of the United States.

Lucretia Mott was a fierce force in the fight for the abolition of slavery and for equality for women.

Though women were permitted to attend the World Anti-Slavery Convention, they could not serve as delegates, nor were they permitted to sit on the main floor of the convention hall. Instead, they were told to sit in a separate area at the end of the hall. They were even forced to sit behind a curtain while the convention took place. To Mott and Cady Stanton, this was an outrage. Women had worked side by side with men as antislavery activists. The women thought they should be permitted to serve as delegates, especially at such an important event.

The convention was not nearly as significant as its delegates hoped it would be. Though its agenda was to end slavery and the slave trade, its primary claim to fame turned out to be the exclusion of women participants. As delegate after delegate rose to defend barring women from participation, Cady Stanton and Mott grew more and more outraged. The two women rose from their seats and stormed out of the convention hall. Cady Stanton would write about this famous London walkout in her memoirs: "As Mrs. Mott and I walked away arm in arm, commenting on the incidents of the day, we resolved to hold a convention as soon as we returned home, and form a society to advocate the rights of women."[1] This conversation proved to be a significant early step toward equal rights. Though Cady Stanton and Mott planned to hold their women's rights convention soon after they returned home from England, the convention itself would have to wait eight years.

The Stantons' Early Life

The Stantons were still a young newlywed couple when they returned to Johnstown, New York, a fact that delayed Cady Stanton's work as a women's rights activist. As soon

The Underground Railroad

In the early 1800s, slavery in America had been legal for two centuries. And slaves had been running away from their owners the entire time. However, where could they go? Antislavery sentiment, gaining momentum after the American Revolution, had resulted in the abolition of slavery in the Northern states by 1805, but the Southern states steadfastly refused, a stubbornness that would result in the Civil War.

By the 1830s, former slaves and abolition activists created a secret network of routes and safe houses known as the Underground Railroad. Not a literal railroad (though sometimes escaping slaves were hidden on railroad cars), it was a sophisticated system that helped slaves escape the South. The most famous Underground Railroad "conductor" was Harriet Tubman (ca. 1820–1913), who escaped slavery in Maryland in 1849. Not content to remain in the safety of the North, she returned to Maryland at least nineteen times to guide slaves to freedom. Like many abolition activists, Tubman was also a strong supporter of the women's rights movement.

as the Stantons got back from Europe, they started a family. Henry became a lawyer, working for a time as Daniel Cady's assistant until he opened his own law practice in Boston in 1842. And just as Henry's career as an attorney began, so did Elizabeth's role as a mother. The Stantons' first child, Daniel Cady Stanton, was born in 1842; their second child, Henry B. Stanton, was born in 1844; and their third child, Gerrit Smith Stanton, was born in 1845.

Cady Stanton thrived in her role as mother, gaining additional confidence. She was also stimulated by the intellectual spirit in Boston. During her years in Boston, Cady Stanton met several famous people: writer and philosopher Ralph Waldo Emerson, novelist Nathaniel Hawthorne, poet John Greenleaf Whittier, composer Stephen Foster, and legendary abolitionist Frederick Douglass. Cady Stanton converted Douglass to the women's rights cause. Years later, Douglass would recall meeting Cady Stanton.

> I shall never forget how she unfolded her views to me on this question of the exclusion of women from having a hand in the governing of herself [...] Mrs. Stanton knew it was not only necessary to break the silence of women and make her voice heard, but woman must have a clear, palpable and comprehensive measure set before her, one worthy of her highest ambition and her best exertions.[2]

While in Boston, Cady Stanton continued her work as an abolitionist, all the while planning to follow up on her desire to hold a women's rights convention. However, two complications arose that further delayed the planned women's rights convention: both Henry Stanton's and Lucretia Mott's health.

Though Henry was thriving as a well-respected Boston attorney, the Massachusetts climate did not agree with him. He was constantly ill with colds and persistent coughs. Though Henry did not wish to leave Boston, his health finally forced him to. In 1845, the Stantons moved to Seneca Falls, New York, a move that would prove beneficial to both Henry and Elizabeth.

Meanwhile, the trip to England had been quite stressful for Lucretia Mott. Upon returning to America, she became sick. According to historian Otelia Cromwell, "A sufferer from chronic dyspepsia [a stomach ailment], she became seriously ill shortly after her return from England; for a time her life was despaired of. As word of her illness spread, grave concern for her health was felt throughout the country."[3]

After several months of rest, Mott finally recovered. But tragedy struck Mott's family soon after her recovery. In 1844, Mott's mother, Anna Coffin, died, and in 1846, her brother, Thomas Coffin, also died. Though Mott was eager to follow up the promises she and Cady Stanton had made in London in 1840, she needed some time to recover.

The Cady Stanton-Mott Partnership

For Mott and Cady Stanton, their dreams of a women's rights convention would come true in 1848. Even at that time, the memories of the women abolitionists' humiliation in London were still fresh in Elizabeth Cady Stanton's mind:

> My experience at the World's Antislavery Convention, all I had read of the legal status of women, and the oppression I saw everywhere, together swept across my soul, intensified now by many personal experiences. It seemed as if all the elements had conspired to impel me to some

> onward step. I could not see what to do or where
> to begin—my only thought was a public meeting
> for protest and discussion.[4]

By 1848, Mott had recovered her strength. In the summer, she was in the middle of an antislavery lecture tour. In the early summer, Cady Stanton received a letter from Martha Wright, Mott's sister, who lived nearby in Auburn, New York. Mott was coming to Auburn, so Wright invited Cady Stanton to visit in July. It had been eight years since Cady Stanton had met Mott, and she was eager to renew their friendship. They arranged a meeting at the home of Jane and Richard Hunt, Quaker friends of the Wrights', who lived in Waterloo, New York. That town was less than 4 miles (6.4 km) from Seneca Falls.

Cady Stanton arrived in Waterloo on Thursday, July 13, 1848. She was delighted to find her dear friend Lucretia in good health, full of enthusiasm and energy. There were five women at the Hunt home that day: Elizabeth Cady Stanton, Lucretia Mott, Martha Wright, Jane Hunt, and Mary McClintock. Though the women were excited to make and renew friendships, the discussion soon focused on Mott and Cady Stanton's experience in London. Wright, Hunt, and McClintock were shocked by the story, and the women renewed Cady Stanton and Mott's original intent to organize a women's rights convention. All agreed that the convention should occur immediately, especially since Mott was in New York. As one of the best-known abolitionists, her famous name would draw people to the convention.

Amazingly, those five women put together the convention in less than a week. They set the dates for the conference to be July 19–20, 1848. The convention was to begin only six days from the meeting at the Hunt home.

Two teams were organized. One group went to the newspaper to take out an advertisement. The other found a location for the conference. They had convinced the minister of the Wesleyan Methodist Church in Seneca Falls to let them use the building for the convention. They also took out a small notice in the local paper, the *Seneca County Courier.*

> A convention to discuss the social, civil and religious condition and rights of woman, will be held in the Wesleyan Chapel, at Seneca Falls, N.Y., on Wednesday and Thursday the 19th and 20th of July current; commencing at 10 o'clock, a.m. During the first day the meeting will be exclusively for women, who are earnestly invited to attend. The public generally are invited to be present on the second day, when Lucretia Mott, of Philadelphia, and other ladies and gentlemen, will address the convention.[5]

Though the women were excited by the upcoming convention, they did not expect a large gathering. It was a hot summer, and Seneca Falls was a long distance from the centers of reform in America, especially New York City, Boston, and Philadelphia. But word of the convention spread quickly, and as July 19 dawned, masses of people descended on the small town of Seneca Falls.

"The Elective Franchise"

The convention began at precisely 10 a.m. Only women were allowed to enter the church, except for Mott's husband, James. In traditional parliamentary procedure, a chairman calls the proceedings to order. Desiring legitimacy for the convention, the women delegates asked James Mott to call the meeting to order.

Dozens of men surrounded the church, peering into the windows and listening at the doors, grumbling at their exclusion. The doors having been ceremoniously locked, Lucretia Mott began reading the convention's Declaration of Sentiments. This document, modeled after the Declaration of Independence, aired the grievances that women had been enduring for centuries. In the Declaration of Independence,

Elizabeth Cady Stanton was one of the organizers of the Women's Convention in Seneca Falls in 1848. She addressed the attendees directly.

the Founding Fathers had written, "We hold these truths to be self-evident: that all men are created equal." The women of the Seneca Falls Convention, however, announced in their declaration, "We hold these truths to be self-evident: that all men and women are created equal." Adding the words "and women" was a bold move, resulting in murmurs of approval from the approximately one hundred women in the church.

What followed in the 976-word Declaration of Sentiments were grievances regarding the historic mistreatment of women and about men's refusal to grant equal treatment to women, who were seen as "the weaker sex." Another grievance read, "He has denied her the facilities for obtaining a thorough education, all colleges being closed against her."[6] As the fifteen grievances were read, a man crawled through one of the church windows and fell into the building. He then unlocked the door, and men filed into the church. Several women demanded that the men leave immediately.

Not wanting to repeat the exclusion that they themselves had suffered for so long, the women ultimately agreed to allow the men to remain. Cady Stanton recalled, "[I]t was decided, in hasty council round the altar, that this was an occasion when men might make themselves pre-eminently useful." Soon, the building was crowded with men and women. They were packed shoulder-to-shoulder in the pews and standing elbow-to-elbow in the aisles. There were too many for the church to accommodate. Many people were still forced to stand outside, hoping to hear the proceedings.

After the Declaration of Sentiments was read, another document was announced: the Resolutions. The purpose of the Declaration was to list the grievances that women had regarding their mistreatment. The purpose of the resolutions was to propose solutions to the grievances. Mott read the twelve resolutions, the first being "Resolved, That such laws as conflict, in any way with the true and substantial happiness of woman, are contrary to the great precept of nature and of no validity, for this is 'superior in obligation to any other.'"

The crowd met all but one of the twelve resolutions with applause and shouts of approval. But when the ninth resolution was read, a hush fell over the crowd: "Resolved, That it is the duty of the women of this country to secure to themselves their sacred right to the elective franchise." Many in the audience—both men and women—opposed the suggestion that women should have "the elective franchise," that is, the right to vote. The momentary silence was broken by Mott, who dutifully read the remaining three resolutions. She then announced that the convention would vote on each resolution the following day.

A break was then announced, and everyone filed out of the church. It was an extraordinary event. Many in the crowd realized that they were on the wave of a revolution. But the real topic of conversation—the real controversy— among the crowd was Resolution 9. The issue of women's suffrage dominated the convention for the remainder of the two-day conference.

As July 19 ended, Cady Stanton grew concerned. She knew that men would be adamantly opposed to women's suffrage, just as men had been opposed to it during the American and French Revolutions. Cady Stanton was shocked that many women at the convention were opposed to women's suffrage as well. She feared that when the

Frederick Douglass was a prolific writer, speaker, and rights activist in the 1800s. His autobiographies are some of the most well-known books from the abolitionist period and pre–Civil War era today.

Frederick Douglass

Because slave births and deaths were not accurately kept, no one knows exactly when Frederick Douglass was born, but it was probably about 1818 in Talbot County, Maryland (on Maryland's eastern shore). The "property" of slaveholder Thomas Auld, the teenager Douglass was loaned out to Hugh Auld (Thomas's brother) in Baltimore, whose wife Sophia secretly taught Douglass the alphabet. (Slaves were forbidden to receive an education.) Knowing only the alphabet, Douglass taught himself how to read and began teaching other slaves as well. Outraged at this news, Thomas Auld sold Douglass to Edward Covey, a Maryland farmer who brutally beat his slaves, Douglass especially. Douglass escaped from the Covey farm, following the Underground Railroad to New York, a free state. He published *Narrative of the Life of Frederick Douglass* in 1845, which became an international sensation. He would become the most important abolitionist in American history and also a tireless advocate for women's suffrage. He died in 1895.

convention voted on the resolutions, Resolution 9 might be rejected, a possibility that filled her with dread. To make matters worse, her own husband was against Resolution 9!

Furthermore, at that time, Cady Stanton did not feel confident as a public speaker. Though she was bold, intelligent, and courageous, she had not yet developed public-speaking skills. Fortunately for the cause of women's suffrage, one of the most famous public speakers in America was at the Seneca Falls Convention—Frederick Douglass. Cady Stanton approached Douglass to ask for help. He had traveled 50 miles (80.5 km) from his home in Rochester, New York, to be involved in this momentous convention, and he was eager to help out. He assured her that when the time came to vote, he would do all he could to secure the passage of Resolution 9.

At 10 a.m. on July 20, the convention resumed. The order of business was to vote first on the Declaration of Sentiments. The women delegates passed it unanimously. Everyone was looking forward to the evening session, when the convention would vote on the resolutions, especially the now-controversial Resolution 9. At 7 p.m., the Wesleyan Methodist Church was packed, with even more people jammed into the building than had been there for the previous session. Everyone knew it was a historic occasion. But were they at the dawn of a new age—when men and women could vote together—or would the old order win the day?

The first eight resolutions passed unanimously. And then Mott began to read Resolution 9 before a crowd hushed in anticipation. According to parliamentary procedure, when a resolution is announced, someone must "make a motion" to adopt the resolution. After that motion, another person has to "second" the motion, meaning that at least two people must approve of the motion before the rest of the people can vote on it. After Resolution 9 was read, Cady Stanton, to no one's surprise, rose to move that the resolution be approved. She then sat down, hoping that someone would rise to second the motion. A long, uncomfortable silence followed.

After a few tense moments, Frederick Douglass slowly rose to second the motion. The crowd was amazed. Douglass, a former slave and an abolitionist speaker, was one of the most famous men in America, and here he was proudly arguing for women to have the right to vote. In his bold, powerful voice, he proclaimed, "The power to choose rulers and make laws is the right by which all others could be secured."[7]

Resolution 9 passed. This was a wonderful moment for Cady Stanton. Eight years earlier, she had been forced to sit mute in the Freemason's Hall in London, unable to speak out against the evils of slavery because she was a woman. And now, a prominent American, Frederick Douglass, had supported the passage of Resolution 9 at the Seneca Falls Convention. At that moment, the partnership of the abolition and women's suffrage movements was solidified. The cause of women's suffrage had made a crucial step forward.

5

SUSAN B. ANTHONY

The passage of the resolutions at the Seneca Falls Convention was an important milestone in the history of women's suffrage. However, women still needed to obtain the right to vote. And they needed more activists to join the fight.

Fortunately for the cause of women's suffrage, a strong wave of activists would come forward after Seneca Falls. Many of them, like Cady Stanton and Mott, came from the abolitionist movement. In 1848, only white men could vote and slavery was still legal, so there was still much work to be done. At the crest of that wave of activism was one of the most important people in American history: Susan B. Anthony.

Early Life

Susan Brownell Anthony was born on February 15, 1820, in Adams, Massachusetts, the third of Daniel and Lucy Anthony's eight children. Like Lucretia Mott, the Anthonys were Quakers and abolitionists. Susan enjoyed a healthy, normal childhood. In 1826, the Anthony family moved to Battenville, New York (about 35 miles [56 km] north of Albany) so that Daniel Anthony could manage a factory.

Susan B. Anthony was a proud advocate for women's rights.

Young Susan was sent to the local district school. Though little was expected of girls academically in those days, Susan was very intelligent and excelled in her studies. She soon proved herself the smartest student in her class. Not long after she started school, however, the teacher refused to teach the girls long division. The teacher insisted that girls were not smart enough to learn such difficult math. Susan stormed home in a fit of anger and told her father.

Susan was fortunate to have a father such as Daniel Anthony, who believed that women were men's equals. Wishing his daughters to receive the best possible education, Daniel Anthony withdrew Susan and her older sister Guelma from the district school and decided to teach his daughters at home. His work as a factory manager was time-consuming, however, so he hired a full-time teacher, Mary Perkins, for the Anthony "home school." Though public schools in America at that time were more interested in teaching "the feminine morality of humility and piety" to girls, Perkins believed that girls should receive the same strict education as boys.[1]

When Susan turned seventeen, she began attending Deborah Moulson's Female Seminary, a Quaker boarding school, near Philadelphia, Pennsylvania. Though the Moulson school, like many "finishing schools," was primarily interested in teaching morality, it nevertheless included rigorous training in algebra, accounting, literature, chemistry, philosophy, and anatomy.

The headmistress, Deborah Moulson, believed that in order for girls to become religious, serious adults, they must be constantly humiliated. Soon after arriving at school, Susan felt the full effect of Moulson's teaching style. One day, Susan had finished a handwriting exercise, and, eager to please Moulson, she rushed up to the front of class to show her the paper. Fully expecting praise for her beautiful, careful handwriting, Susan instead heard Moulson say, "Obviously, Susan, you do not know the rule for dotting 'i's. I have devoted my time to you in vain."[2] Susan was crushed and returned to her desk.

Susan suffered more such humiliations. But life was not always miserable for Susan at school. She was fortunate to make friends with Lydia Mott, the niece of Lucretia Mott. Because Lydia was a student at Moulson, her famous aunt often came to the school to lecture the girls on intellectual development and civic responsibility. Lucretia Mott's lectures, filled with hope and respect, were quite different than the oppressive style of Moulson. They impressed the young mind of Susan Anthony, who by then was growing more sensitive to issues of social justice.

Susan did not endure the harsh environment of Moulson for long. Before her first year was finished, Susan was called home. A financial crisis had gripped the nation in 1837, and the Anthony home was one of its victims. Daniel Anthony had suffered financial ruin and could no longer afford Susan's schooling.

Anthony and Activism

To help pay off her father's massive debts, Susan B. Anthony became a schoolteacher. In 1839, she took her first job at Kenyon's Friends' Seminary, a Quaker school in New Rochelle, New York. The headmistress, Eunice Kenyon, was an easy-going, cheerful woman—a stark contrast to Deborah Moulson. Kenyon urged Anthony to explore her own style of teaching. New Rochelle was not far from New

York City, and Anthony occasionally went to the city to attend temperance or abolition lectures.

In 1846, the twenty-six-year-old Anthony took a position as headmistress of girls' education at the Canajoharie Academy in Canajoharie, New York. The town was halfway between Albany and Utica. Anthony was a good teacher. She demanded a lot from her students, but she did not believe in the berating, humiliating style of Deborah Moulson. She taught the same subjects as were taught at Moulson but in the more easy-going style learned from Kenyon.

While living in Canajoharie, Anthony began her career as an activist. Canajoharie was not far from the home of her old school friend, Lydia Mott, who lived with her sister Abigail in Albany. Anthony often visited the Mott sisters, who, because of their connection to their famous aunt, were actively involved in various reform movements. In 1848, the New York Property Bill was amended to allow women partial property rights. Although the Mott sisters were excited by this monumental reform in the New York legal system, they believed it was only a start toward larger, more dramatic reforms. That summer was also the summer of the Seneca Falls Convention, which had brought recognition to Lucretia Mott and Elizabeth Cady Stanton. At the Mott home, Anthony would meet many of the pioneers of the women's rights movement.

Soon after arriving in town, Anthony joined an organization called the Daughters of Temperance. Temperance was a reform movement that sought to reduce the consumption of alcoholic beverages.

Though a newcomer to town, Anthony quickly proved herself a likable, confident, and energetic member and rose quickly to the office of secretary. More important, it was as

The History of Woman Suffrage

One of the most important books in American history is *The History of Woman Suffrage*, a six-volume work of more than fifty-seven hundred pages. It is an encyclopedic, painstaking document of the struggle for American women to win the right to vote. Susan B. Anthony, Elizabeth Cady Stanton, and Matilda Joslyn Gage began writing it in 1876. At first, they imagined that it would take a few months to write, but as their research progressed, they realized what a monumental undertaking it was going to be. Ultimately, it would take more than forty-five years to complete, one-third of it written after the deaths of Anthony, Gage, and Cady Stanton. Volumes 5 to 6 were primarily written by Ida Husted Harper (1851–1931) between 1900 and 1920. The book was dedicated to nineteen women, the first one being Mary Wollstonecraft.

a member of the Daughters of Temperance that Anthony began to make her reputation as a bold, forceful public speaker. On March 1, 1849, the Daughters of Temperance invited all the townspeople to attend a formal dinner. Anthony was the featured speaker.

In the nineteenth century, it was rare for a woman to speak in public. Women public speakers were often openly ridiculed by men during their speeches and then subject to further insult in the following days' newspapers. But standing before the two hundred audience members that

Many women who advocated for women's rights were also activists in the temperance movement, made up of people who wanted to stop the sale and consumption of alcohol.

evening, Anthony showed no sign of nerves or fear. Her speech was a rousing success. Both men and women cheered her afterward, hailing Anthony as "the smartest woman who has ever been in Canajoharie."

Anthony had found her activist calling. One month later, she resigned from the Canajoharie Academy and moved back to Rochester. She continued her work as a temperance activist and enlisted in the abolition cause as well. Rochester was not only the home of the Anthony family; it was also the home of Frederick Douglass. Douglass's antislavery newspaper, *The North Star*, was published in Rochester. The city was a stop along the Underground Railroad, with an estimated one hundred fifty escaped slaves coming through town each year. Anthony's father introduced her to Douglass soon after her arrival. They became instant friends and would remain so for the rest of their lives. Impressed by the larger-than-life Douglass, Anthony soon joined the American Anti-Slavery Society.

In the spring of 1851, Anthony traveled to Syracuse, New York, to attend an antislavery convention. On her way back to Rochester, Amelia Bloomer, a fellow temperance activist, invited Anthony to visit her home in Seneca Falls. The town had gained notoriety since the famous convention three years earlier. As a result, it was a popular stop on various lecture tours. That spring, two famous abolitionists, American William Lloyd Garrison and Englishman George Thompson, would deliver antislavery lectures at Seneca Falls. Also attending the lectures was a woman who would forever change Anthony's life: Elizabeth Cady Stanton.

Frederick Douglass had spoken warmly about Cady Stanton, and Anthony was eager to meet her. And there on the street, after the evening's lectures, Bloomer introduced Cady Stanton to Anthony. In her memoirs, Cady Stanton recalled her first impression of Anthony: "There she stood with her good, earnest face and genial smile."[3] They could not have foreseen it at the time, but this introduction would blossom into one of the most famous friendships in American history.

Despite their now-famous meeting in 1851, Anthony and Cady Stanton did not become close friends until several months later. At that time, the two women met with Lucy Stone in order to make plans for a coeducational college in New York. Like Anthony and Cady Stanton, Stone was a tireless advocate for abolition and women's rights.

One of nine children, Lucy Stone was born on August 13, 1818, on a farm near West Brookfield, Massachusetts. As a teenager, she learned that Oberlin College in Ohio would be the first American college to admit women students. Receiving no help from her parents, Stone saved for nine years to attend Oberlin. She became one of the first women in the United States to earn a college degree, graduating in 1847. Though Cady Stanton had become widely known because of the Seneca Falls Convention, it was Lucy Stone

The Grimké Sisters

Two of the nineteen women to whom *The History of Woman Suffrage* is dedicated are Sarah Moore Grimké (1792–1873) and Angelina Emily Grimké (1805–1879), daughters of John Faucheraud Grimké (1752–1819), who was the head judge of the South Carolina Supreme Court after the American Revolution. He was also a prominent landowner and slaveholder. The Grimké sisters were given the standard education for daughters of the Charleston elite—music, sewing, and painting—but they wanted the same education that their brother Thomas (who went to Yale) had, so he taught them subjects such as Greek, Latin, and math. In secret, the girls taught their father's slaves to read and became intimately aware of the horrors of slavery. Sarah and Angelina became Quakers in the 1820s and passionate antislavery activists, organizing the New York Anti-Slavery Convention of American Women in 1837. During the 1830s, the Grimké sisters became aware of the connection between the mistreatment of slaves and the mistreatment of women, so they became women's rights activists as well. In 1837, Sarah published a pamphlet, *Letters on the Equality of the Sexes*, which argued that woman was "in all respects [man's] equal."

Lucy Stone organized the first national women's rights convention in 1850. She also formed a close friendship with Susan B. Anthony and Elizabeth Cady Stanton.

who organized the first national women's rights convention, held in Worcester, Massachusetts, in 1850.

As these three women—Anthony, Cady Stanton, and Stone—sat in the parlor of the Stanton home, they were doing more than making plans to bring college education to New York women. They were laying the foundation for women's suffrage in America.

Though the women were unsuccessful in their attempts to launch a New York coeducational college, those meetings solidified the friendship among the three women. Anthony and Cady Stanton, in fact, became best friends and forged a bond that would ultimately help bring the right to vote to American women.

African American Women Strengthen the Movement

The 1850s were a difficult time in American history. There were growing tensions between the free Northern states and the slaveholding Southern states. Slave owners in the South, who held a large amount of political power, were angry that so many slaves were escaping to the North. Not wanting civil war to erupt, Congress intervened in 1850. The government enacted the Fugitive Slave Law as part of a larger compromise known as the Compromise of 1850. The Fugitive Slave Law called for Northern law officials to return runaway slaves to the South. Immediately after the passage of the law, thousands of former slaves—many of whom had been in the North for years—were rounded up and sent back to their former owners.

With the enactment of the Fugitive Slave Law, abolitionists and women's rights advocates saw more clearly the need to be unified in their efforts. Slavery, after all, was not limited to men. African American women were just as interested in women's rights as they were in abolition. This bond would draw together white and black abolitionists to form a powerful partnership in the struggle for women's rights. The Fugitive Slave Law, which was seen as a shocking violation of human rights, drew together the circles of abolition and women's rights activists.

One of the early leaders of that partnership was the former slave Sojourner Truth. Born into slavery as Isabella Baumfree in Swartekill, New York, about 1797, she was sold as a slave three times before escaping to freedom in 1826. In 1843, she changed her name to Sojourner Truth and began her career as an abolitionist and women's rights activist. Unlike many white women activists, Truth was very poor and had to support herself as a domestic servant while she traveled from town to town. She cleaned homes during the day and delivered abolition lectures in the evenings. People often fiercely opposed her lectures. Not only was it rare for a woman to speak publicly, but an African American woman faced the double hurdles of racism and misogyny (the hatred of women). Many times during her lectures, Truth's voice was drowned out by boos, catcalls, and racist insults. Those same crowds, however, were often won over by her courage and powerful speaking style. By 1851, she had published her autobiography, *The Narrative of Sojourner Truth: A Northern Slave*, and enjoyed the well-earned reputation as a great public speaker.

Sojourner Truth was not alone in her efforts as an African American woman activist. Harriet Forten Purvis and Margaretta Forten, the daughters of a wealthy Philadelphia merchant, James Forten, were influential abolitionists and women's rights activists who helped found the interracial Philadelphia Female Anti-Slavery Society. Mary Ann Shadd

Sojourner Truth faced hardships as an activist during the 1800s, but today she is remembered as one of the greatest speakers and advocates in American history.

Cary founded the abolition newspaper *The Provincial Freeman* in 1853. Sarah Parker Remond was a brilliant woman who, because of racial and sexist prejudice in America, had to travel to Italy to earn her medical degree. She was a strong speaker at many of the women's rights conventions. The 1850s were a vibrant time for the growing women's rights movement. It was clear that the causes of abolition and women's suffrage were linked hand-in-hand. It was also clear that the African American voice was crucial in the fight for women's suffrage.

Many African American abolitionists and women's rights activists were frustrated by racial prejudice within the women's rights movement. To many white activists, women's rights meant white women's rights.[4] Susan B. Anthony, however, saw her African American colleagues as full partners. In a famous incident in 1861, Anthony and Frederick Douglass together hung a large banner from the Rochester Corinthian Hall that read "No compromise with slaveholders."[5] This slogan served as a rallying cry for the abolition cause and also drew thousands of men and women—both black and white—into the women's suffrage cause.

6

THE FIFTEENTH AMENDMENT

The partnership between universal suffrage and abolition achieved victory immediately following the end of the Civil War. On December 6, 1865, Congress ratified the Thirteenth Amendment, which formally abolished slavery.

It was, indeed, a great victory, but, curiously, that amendment did not grant African Americans the right to vote. So the abolition/women's rights partnership still had work to do: the next order of business was to amend the Constitution so that African Americans could vote. But did that mean all African Americans, or just African American men? Because women had been such powerful figures in the abolitionist movement, it was hoped that any new constitutional amendment including African Americans would also include women as voters.

In 1866, Susan B. Anthony, Elizabeth Cady Stanton, Lucy Stone, and Frederick Douglass organized the American Equal Rights Association (AERA). The stated agenda of the AERA was gender and racial equality. One of the AERA's projects was to make sure that suffrage was granted to African Americans but also to make sure any constitutional amendment would also include women.

In February 1869, Congress proposed the Fifteenth Amendment to the US Constitution: "The right of citizens of the United States to vote shall not be denied or abridged by the United States or any State on account of race, color or condition of previous servitude." Though this was hailed as a victory in the African American community, women's rights activists were stunned. Why wasn't "or gender" added to the list of categories not to be denied? The Fifteenth Amendment, in other words, was, if ratified, going to grant suffrage to African American men but not to any women.

The AERA, at its third-anniversary convention in May 1869, met in New York to discuss the Fifteenth Amendment. Douglass, much to the surprise of many of the women present, made a resolution to "welcome the pending Fifteenth Amendment prohibiting disenfranchisement on account of race and earnestly solicit the State legislatures to pass it without delay."[1] Many of the African American women present at the convention felt betrayed. The proposed amendment would exclude them from suffrage because of their gender. Despite this, Douglass believed that it was better to grant suffrage only to African American men than to have no constitutional amendment at all. Anthony rose to protest the resolution:

> The business of this association is to demand for every man, black or white, and every woman, black or white, that they shall be enfranchised and admitted into the body politic with equal rights and privileges.[2]

After much heated debate, the AERA voted to support Douglass's resolution. This outraged many of the women present. On the very last day of the convention, the Woman's Bureau of the AERA met to discuss these controversial events. Many of them wanted no further part of the AERA. They felt that women, who had been among the most loyal crusaders in the abolitionist movement, were now being left out of the reforms once slavery had been abolished.

At that meeting, held on May 15, 1869, Susan B. Anthony, Elizabeth Cady Stanton, and Lucy Stone formed the National Woman Suffrage Association (NWSA). They launched a nationwide lecture tour, hoping to rally support to pressure Congress to include women in the Fifteenth

The Revolution

In 1868, Susan B. Anthony, Elizabeth Cady Stanton, and Parker Pillsbury (1809–1898), a famous abolitionist and women's suffrage advocate, founded their own reform newspaper, the *Revolution*. It was published weekly between January 8, 1868, and February 17, 1872. Its motto was "Principle, not Policy; Justice, not Favors." An annual subscription cost two dollars. The first article in Issue 1, penned by Cady Stanton herself, began with: "The Question of the enfranchisement of women has already passed the court of moral discussion, and is now fairly ushered into the arena of politics, where it must remain a fixed element of debate, until party necessity shall compel its success." Together with the AERA, the *Revolution* pressured the US Congress to include women in the Fifteenth Amendment.

The National Woman Suffrage Association was one organization
taking the idea of women's voting rights seriously.

Amendment. Anthony and Cady Stanton's newspaper, the *Revolution*, continued to carry articles about women's suffrage. Thousands of men and women wrote letters of protest to their congressmen, and the lecture tour rallied support for the women's suffrage cause.

But not everyone present at the birth of the NWSA was happy. Believing that the NWSA was too radical, Lucy Stone withdrew from the organization and formed the American Woman Suffrage Association (AWSA) in November 1869. The AWSA believed that women's suffrage could be achieved through federalism rather than through a constitutional amendment. In other words, the AWSA thought that if they could convince individual states to adopt women's suffrage first, then nationwide suffrage would happen eventually. In her initial letter to form the AWSA, Stone wrote:

> The undersigned, being convinced of the necessity for an American Woman Suffrage Association, which shall embody the deliberate action of the State organizations, and shall carry with it their united weight, do hereby respectfully invite such organizations to be represented in a Delegate Convention.[3]

Stone was concerned that there was too much bitterness between Southern congressmen, who rabidly opposed the Fifteenth Amendment, and Northern congressmen, many of whom had been involved in abolitionist movements. With so much infighting in the halls of the US Congress, Stone believed that the best chance for women's suffrage would be to pressure individual state legislatures—the Northern states first, of course—to adopt women's suffrage. The highest-profile members of the AWSA were Lucy Stone; her husband, Henry Blackwell; author Julia Ward Howe; and Henry Ward Beecher, the AWSA's first president.

On February 3, 1870, the Fifteenth Amendment to the US Constitution was ratified. African American men were now "enfranchised"; for the first time, they could vote. The abolitionist movement had succeeded—slavery was outlawed and African American men could vote. Nevertheless, hopes that women's suffrage would be part of the post-abolition reforms were dashed. It was a devastating setback. However, because of the formation of the NWSA and the AWSA, a wave of public support for women's suffrage began to build.

"Lucy Stoners"

In 1855, Lucy Stone married the antislavery activist Henry Blackwell. The marriage became a national scandal when Stone refused to adopt her husband's last name. Even though there was no law requiring a wife to take her husband's last name, Stone nevertheless was forced to sign legal documents as "Lucy Stone, wife of Henry Blackwell." For decades afterwards, married women who kept their maiden names were known as "Lucy Stoners." In 1921, the American writer Ruth Hale founded the Lucy Stone League, a women's rights organization whose motto was "A wife should no more take her husband's name than he should hers. My name is my identity and must not be lost."[4]

One of the first radical steps occurred in 1872, the presidential election year following the passage of the Fifteenth Amendment. Stifled by the Fifteenth Amendment, Susan B. Anthony attempted to challenge a clause in the Fourteenth Amendment in order to vote in the election. On the morning of November 1, 1872, in Rochester, Anthony marched with her two sisters, Guelma McLean and Hannah Mosher, to the voter registration station at the local barbershop. The men at the registration table glared at the women. "I demand that you register us as voters," said Anthony calmly. The men refused.

"If you still refuse us our rights as citizens," Anthony said, standing her ground, "I will bring charges against you in Criminal Court and I will sue each of you personally for large, exemplary damages."[5]

The men still turned Anthony and her sisters away. But three days later, Anthony and fourteen other women snuck into the voting station and cast their ballots. Three weeks later, Anthony was arrested for illegal voting. It was an international sensation. Newspapers all across the country described Anthony's attempt to vote. The *New York Times* headline blazed "Female Suffrage—The Case of Miss Anthony."[6] The news crossed the Atlantic Ocean. The *London Times* ran a story on "the conviction of Miss Susan B. Anthony, a famous advocate of Women's Rights, of having violated the election laws by voting in the November election."[7]

Anthony's goal in attempting to vote in the 1872 election was to "invoke" the first paragraph of the Fourteenth Amendment to the US Constitution, which granted full citizenship to anyone "born or naturalized in the United States." If American women were "born" in America, shouldn't they be granted a citizenship right such as the right to vote? Anthony was indeed hoping to be arrested. If she were convicted of illegal voting in the New York courts, then she could appeal the ruling to the Supreme Court. The US Supreme Court is the highest court in the country. But the New York Supreme Court prevented her from taking her case to the US Supreme Court. This was another bitter blow to the women's suffrage movement. Because the Fourteenth Amendment would not get challenged in the Supreme Court, a new constitutional amendment would have to be sought. After 1872, Anthony marched to the halls of Congress almost every year to demand a Sixteenth Amendment: "The rights of citizens of the United States to vote shall not be denied or abridged by the United States or any State on account of sex." Anthony and others were finally able to persuade Congress to vote on the amendment in 1887, though it was defeated.

Meanwhile, Lucy Stone and the AWSA were working to pressure individual states to legalize women's suffrage, with little success. For the next several years, the NWSA and AWSA worked independently to bring women's suffrage to America. But there was a growing sentiment that if the movement were to succeed, it could only happen if women were united.

In 1890, Elizabeth Cady Stanton turned seventy-five, Susan B. Anthony turned seventy, and Lucy Stone turned seventy-two. Anthony and Cady Stanton felt betrayed by Stone when she left the NWSA in 1869, and the tensions between the women lasted a long time. For the women's suffrage movement to move forward, those old wounds would have to be healed. To bring the two organizations together, Harriot Stanton Blatch (Cady Stanton's daughter),

Alice Stone Blackwell (Lucy Stone's daughter), and others organized a convention, to be held in Washington, DC. In February 1890, the AWSA and NWSA met there to unite the two organizations. At that point, the National American Woman Suffrage Association (NAWSA) was born. In many ways, it was the passing of the reins to a new generation of women's suffrage activists. No one could adequately fill the roles of Anthony, Cady Stanton, and Stone, who had worked tirelessly for decades and had become significant reformers in American history. But the movement was entering a new phase, and younger women were needed to finish the work their mothers had begun.

That same year, 1890, the Wyoming Territory, the first territory to legalize women's suffrage, entered the Union with women's suffrage still intact as the forty-fourth state. By 1900, Colorado, Utah, and Idaho also approved women's suffrage. Some states were legalizing women's suffrage, but there was still no federal law giving women the vote.

African American Women Organize

In the nineteenth century, there was perhaps no group of people in the United States more united in the causes of abolition and suffrage than African American women. African American women had actually experienced the double sting of slavery and antisuffrage. Beginning in the 1880s, African American women began organizing local suffrage groups. Mary Ann Shadd Cary, publisher of the abolition journal *The Provincial Freeman*, founded the Colored Women's Progressive Franchise Association, based in Washington, DC, in 1880. The organization's three foundations were "Demand equal rights," "Reject the idea

Harriet Tubman helped found the National Association of Colored Women in 1896.

Margaret Murray Washington was the wife of Booker T. Washington and a supporter of African American women's rights.

that only men conduct industrial and other enterprises," and "Obtain the ballot."[8]

Soon, other organizations appeared, such as the National Association of Colored Women (founded by Harriet Tubman, Frances E. W. Harper, Ida Bell Wells-Barnett, and Mary Church Terrell in 1896). Margaret Murray Washington, wife of African American activist Booker T. Washington, founded the National Federation of Afro American Women. Not just interested in women's suffrage, these organizations were active in fighting alcoholism and racism (especially strong in the American South, where lynchings were commonplace). These and many other local organizations brought together tens of thousands of African Americans to fight for equality.

7

VICTORY

As the twentieth century approached its second decade, the three great heroes of the women's suffrage movement—Cady Stanton, Stone, and Anthony—were gone. To the sadness and frustration of tens of thousands of suffrage activists, the "Big Three" of women's suffrage died before women won the right to vote. Lucy Stone died in 1893 at the age of seventy-five; Elizabeth Cady Stanton at seventy-seven in 1902; and Susan B. Anthony at eighty-six in 1906. But they had planted a tree that would ultimately bear fruit.

A final push was needed to legalize women's suffrage. Fortunately, there were, at the turn of the twentieth century, legions of women now committed to the cause. This new generation had the energy and dedication to finish the job.

Anti-Women's Suffrage Activists

After the Civil War, the cult of domesticity began to lose its hold on the American imagination. The "true woman" was being replaced by the "new woman." The "true woman" had to stay at home, but the "new woman" now had more opportunities. No longer confined to the home, the "new woman" could seek fulfillment in other arenas. More and more women were becoming doctors, lawyers, and professors. Men had traditionally held these careers.

But not everyone welcomed the "new woman." There were still many people in America who longed for the days when women "knew their place," that is, in the home. Many saw the "new woman" as a threat to the traditional way of life. And to them, perhaps the biggest threat was women's suffrage. As a result of this fear, many antisuffrage organizations began to appear.

Surprisingly, many women—in addition to men— were involved in the antisuffrage movement. Just three years after the Seneca Falls Convention, in 1851, Mrs. Albert T. Leatherbee of Boston published *The Anti-Suffrage Campaign Manual.* In it, she argued that women's suffrage "will not be a progressive step, but a retrogressive one."[1]

In 1872, one thousand people signed a petition to the US Congress to deny the vote to women. Two of the most high-profile signers of that petition were wives of famous Civil War officers: Eleanor Sherman, wife of General William Sherman, and Madeleine Dahlgren, wife of Admiral John Dahlgren.[2] Afterward, antisuffrage organizations began to appear, including the Massachusetts Anti-Suffrage Committee, the National Association Opposed to Woman Suffrage, and the Women's National Anti-Suffrage League. There was even an antisuffrage newspaper, *The Remonstrance*, which operated from 1890 to 1908. Suffragettes were caricatured in local and national media, and often taunted and humiliated in public. According to the historian Susan Goodier, "When some women began

This cartoon was displayed on a postcard in Britain in the 1900s. Other similar antisuffrage materials made their rounds in the United Kingdom and the United States during this time.

agitating for the right to vote in the 1840s, most observers expressed revulsion, contempt, or disbelief."[3]

Many historians note that most women who opposed women's suffrage were wealthy and feared that women's suffrage would threaten their privileged position in society. But there were other factors as well. The Southern states were afraid that giving the vote to black women, as well as to black men (the Fifteenth Amendment), would threaten Southern white supremacy. In addition, American alcohol interests feared that, because so many American women were involved in temperance organizations, granting women's suffrage might result in a ban on alcoholic drinks.

This threat against alcohol interests ensured that anti-women's suffrage organizations were very well financed. The alcohol companies spared no expense in fighting women's suffrage.[4] According to Eileen L. McDonagh and H. Douglas Price, "The presumed alliance between the woman suffrage movement and the Prohibition movement cost the suffrage movement dearly, as the suffrage cause automatically inherited the enemies of Prohibition, most notably, the brewing interests."[5]

But perhaps the most powerful opponent of women's suffrage after the turn of the twentieth century was Woodrow Wilson, the twenty-eighth president of the United States. By the time he became president in 1913, the women's suffrage movement had made great strides toward earning women the vote, but Wilson fiercely opposed women's suffrage. He was "the principle antagonist in the final chapter of the long battle for suffrage."[6] Would anyone be able to challenge such a powerful man? Fortunately for the women's suffrage cause, one woman who rose to the challenge was Alice Paul.

Alice Paul: A New Leader

Alice Paul was born in 1885 in New Jersey, and, like women's rights pioneers Lucretia Mott and Susan B. Anthony, she was a Quaker. However, unlike Anthony and Mott, Paul was born at a time when there were far more educational and professional opportunities available to women. Of course, those new opportunities were due in large part to the work of Mott and Anthony. Paul was the oldest of four children born to William and Tacie Paul. William Paul was a successful banker who supported Alice in her educational ambitions. Alice went to a Quaker

Alice Paul was a Quaker who worked hard to achieve women's rights in the United States.

school as a child and then to Swarthmore College, where she majored in biology. A brilliant student, Alice Paul continued her education after Swarthmore, ultimately earning a doctorate in sociology from the University of Pennsylvania. She also studied economics and politics in England and earned a law degree from American University in Washington, DC. She was, during her lifetime, one of the most educated women in history.

It was during her studies in England that Paul became a women's suffrage advocate. Walking along London streets in 1907, Paul stumbled on a small crowd gathered around a

The Pankhursts

A major influence on the final push toward American women's suffrage was Englishwoman Emmeline Pankhurst (1858–1928) and her two daughters, Christabel (1880–1958) and Estelle (1882–1960). Emmeline organized the Women's Social and Political Union (WSPU) in 1903 to promote women's suffrage in England. When the British government ignored the WSPU's polite efforts to gain the vote, the organization resorted to more radical methods. WSPU members staged street rallies, broke into government meetings, and committed many acts of civil disobedience, including hunger strikes, to gain publicity for women's suffrage. Between 1907 and 1914, the Pankhursts were arrested many times, often enduring beatings and force-feedings. England granted women the right to vote in 1918.

Emmeline Pankhurst was a leader in the fight for women's suffrage in Britain. Her efforts and those of others began as peaceful but turned defiant and dangerous as the years progressed.

woman arguing for British women's suffrage. That woman was Christabel Pankhurst, daughter of the most famous women's suffrage activist in England, Emmeline Pankhurst.

Paul befriended the Pankhursts and joined the Women's Social and Political Union (WSPU), the organization fighting for women's suffrage in England. On two occasions, Paul was arrested and jailed while participating in women's suffrage protests. During her second imprisonment, a thirty-day jail sentence, Paul refused to eat—a strategy known as a hunger strike—in order to call attention to women's suffrage. She also wanted to shame the police into releasing her early. She was not released early, however. Instead, she was force-fed, a painful process in which a tube was stuck down her throat to give her liquid food. When the twenty-five-year-old Paul returned to the United States in 1910, she was in poor health from her grueling experience in England. But she was ready to fight for women's suffrage in the same way that Pankhurst was fighting in England. After completing her doctoral studies in 1912, Paul joined the National American Woman Suffrage Association (NAWSA).

The women's suffrage movement needed Paul's energy. Since the deaths of Anthony, Cady Stanton, and Stone, the movement had stalled, entering a phase historians today call "the doldrums."[7] The president of the NAWSA since 1904 had been Dr. Anna Howard Shaw. American suffragists greatly admired Shaw, a powerful public speaker. However, she was making little headway toward gaining a constitutional suffrage amendment. The NAWSA put Paul in charge of the Congressional Committee, whose job was to fight for a constitutional amendment. Paul knew that what was needed was a big splash.

The Women's Suffrage Parade

That splash came on March 3, 1913, the day before Woodrow Wilson was inaugurated as president. Bringing together thousands of people dedicated to women's suffrage, Paul organized the Women's Suffrage Parade. Starting at the Capitol building, eight thousand marchers headed up Pennsylvania Avenue, passing the White House, and ending at the Hall of the Daughters of the American Revolution.

Inez Milholland

At the front of the Women's Suffrage Parade, wearing a crown, a white dress, and a white cape was Inez Milholland (1886–1916), a twenty-seven-year-old suffragist. In 1907, after her sophomore year at Vassar College, in Poughkeepise, New York, Milholland traveled to London, where she met the Pankhursts, who recruited her to the Women's Social and Political Union, participating in several of their demonstrations. Returning to Vassar that fall and, despite the college's policy forbidding any discussion of women's suffrage, Milholland organized the Vassar Votes for Women Club. After graduating from Vassar, she was rejected by the Harvard, Yale, and Columbia law schools because of her sex. However, she was accepted to New York University School of Law, receiving her degree in 1912. A tireless women's suffrage and anti-war activist, Milholland died tragically of pernicious anemia after giving a suffrage lecture in Los Angeles in 1916.

Many suffragettes marched in Washington, DC, in 1913.

At the head of the parade, sitting boldly atop a white horse, was Inez Milholland, who carried a purple, white, and gold banner. The banner colors were "purple for the royal glory of women, white for purity at home and in politics, gold for the crown of the victor."[8]

Soon after the parade began, however, things turned ugly. Men in the crowd hurled insults at the women, telling them to go back home where they belonged. The hecklers also targeted the men who marched with the women, shouting, "Henpecko" and "Where are your skirts?"[9] Soon the mob was hurling objects at the marchers, blocking their pathway and finally attacking them. Though police were there to keep order, they did nothing as the marchers were assaulted. The attackers injured hundreds of marchers. There was a massive public outcry because of the violence. The tide was turning in the suffragists' favor. But Wilson, who was to become president the next day, was unmoved.

Not everyone in the NAWSA was happy with Paul's energetic style. The president of the NAWSA, Dr. Anna Howard Shaw, believed that the quickest path to gaining nationwide suffrage was to petition the individual states. (This had been Lucy Stone's strategy, too.) But between 1869 and 1913, only nine states had adopted women's suffrage, all of them western states far from the nation's capital. The new generation of suffragists, led by Paul, did not want to wait for state-by-state suffrage, a process that might take decades, especially in the American South. The new generation of suffragists wanted a constitutional amendment now. But unfortunately, in early 1914, Shaw and her supporters expelled Paul from the NAWSA.

Undaunted, Paul organized her own suffrage organization, the Congressional Union (CU). The CU traveled the nation, recruiting men and women to the cause. Based on her aggressive efforts, Paul managed to convince the US House of Representatives to vote on a suffrage amendment in 1914. The vote failed, 204 to 174, but the closeness of the vote gave women hope that a constitutional amendment would eventually pass.

President Woodrow Wilson had a change in heart by 1916. Though he had been strongly against women's suffrage during his first term, he gradually began to warm to the idea. While campaigning for a second four-year presidential term, President Wilson told an audience that he supported a suffrage amendment: "We feel the tide; we rejoice in the strength of it, and we shall not quarrel in the long run as to the method of it."[10] Soon, the suffragists' time would come.

Wilson won reelection in November 1916, and the suffragists were convinced that the president was now on their side. But when Congress did not immediately pass a suffrage amendment, the suffragists took to the picket lines again. In early 1917, Paul's CU members stood outside the White House gates, many holding signs that read "Mr. President, What Will You Do for Woman's Suffrage?" and "How Long Must Women Wait for Liberty?"[11] Though President Wilson by then had formally announced his support of women's suffrage, no congressional vote would occur until early 1918. On January 10, 1918, the House of Representatives voted on the "Susan B. Anthony Amendment," that is, an amendment granting women the right to vote. And, finally, the amendment passed 274 to 136. But the passage of the "Anthony Amendment" in the House of Representatives did not grant women the right to vote. It would still have to pass in the US Senate in order for it to become law. It was a slow process, and women would have to wait a year and a half for the Senate to pass the amendment.

The problem was that in order for a constitutional amendment to pass, it had to receive a two-thirds majority in the Senate. On its first vote in January 1918, the amendment passed sixty-two to thirty-four. It was a majority, but it was two votes short of the mandatory two-thirds majority. Suffrage would have to wait another year.

In 1919, the two-thirds majority necessary to pass a constitutional amendment in Congress had been achieved. Though Congress was filled primarily with men, generations of women's suffrage activism had managed to convince most of them that women had now earned the right to vote. On June 4, 1919, Congress officially approved the "Anthony Amendment," fifty-six votes for and twenty-five votes against.

The next step was ratification. Three-fourths of the state legislatures had to approve the amendment. The Nineteenth Amendment to the United States Constitution was officially ratified on August 18, 1920. Entering the US Constitution would be the following law: "The right of citizens of the United States to vote shall not be denied or abridged by the United States or by any State on account of sex." Thanks to the pioneering work of thousands of women's rights advocates during almost two centuries, American women now had the right to vote.

CONCLUSION

In his most famous passage in the Declaration of Independence, Thomas Jefferson wrote, "We hold these truths to be self-evident, that all men are created equal." He wrote those words to King George III, who ruled England, a nation built on inequality. Americans are justifiably proud of these valiant, bold words. They provided the blueprint for a new nation, the United States of America, which would rest on a foundation of freedom and equality. However, as John Adams would remind his wife, Abigail, when she urged him to "remember the ladies," those words applied only to men. Bearing witness to this fact is that, before the ratification of the Nineteenth Amendment in 1920, the United States Constitution did not even include the word "women."

The story of women's suffrage in America is a story of courage, tragedy, heartbreak, patience, and finally, triumph. The nineteenth-century suffrage pioneers fought for voting rights against seemingly insurmountable odds. Lucy Stone, the founder of the American Woman Suffrage Association, saved pennies and nickels for nine years before she was able to go to Oberlin College, the first college in America to admit women students. Sojourner Truth, a slave who had escaped

Today, the women's suffrage movement's legacy continues. Here, these women cast their vote wearing suffragette costumes.

her captors while carrying her infant daughter in 1826, cleaned white people's homes in order to make enough money to give her famous "Ain't I a Woman?" speech. In 1872, Susan B. Anthony, alongside fifteen other suffrage activists, was arrested for attempting to vote in Rochester, New York, which at that time was a federal crime. By

1910, tens of thousands of women, known as "Antis," were members of antisuffrage organizations.

Many activists had to struggle against their own communities and their own families in order to "get the vote." For centuries, women were under the strict control of men. Women were excluded from education, most forms of employment, government, and legal rights. Furthermore, that exclusion existed all over the world. So when women gained the right to vote, they knew that, in many ways, their fight had just begun. Like men, they, too, wanted to live in a world in which they could have the freedom to be whatever they wanted to be. In 1776, John Adams famously told his wife, Abigail, that the Declaration of Independence pertained only to men. But Abigail Adams, Olympe de Gouges, Mary Wollstonecraft, Sojourner Truth, Elizabeth Cady Stanton, Susan B. Anthony, Lucy Stone, and Inez Millholland knew better—they knew what women today know: given the chance, they could prove that all people are created equal.

CHRONOLOGY

1776 The Declaration of Independence is signed by the Founding Fathers; Abigail Adams writes to husband, John Adams, to "remember the ladies."

1789 The French Revolution begins; *The Declaration of the Rights of Man* is published; the US Constitution is ratified; the Women's March to Versailles takes place.

1791 Olympe de Gouges writes *The Declaration of the Rights of Woman.*

1792 Mary Wollstonecraft writes *A Vindication of the Rights of Woman.*

1793 Lucretia Mott is born in Nantucket, Massachusetts, on January 3.

1814 Esther Morris is born in Oswego, New York, on August 8.

1815 Elizabeth Cady Stanton is born in Johnstown, New York, on November 12.

1818 Lucy Stone is born near West Brookfield, Massachusetts, on August 13.

1820 Susan B. Anthony is born in Adams, Massachusetts, on February 15.

1821 The Troy Female Seminary opens.

1837 Oberlin College becomes the first college in the United States to admit women; Mount Holyoke Female Seminary opens as the first American college for women only.

1840 Women are denied participation at the World Anti-Slavery Convention in London.

1848 The Seneca Falls Convention is held.

1850 The first national women's rights convention is held in Worcester, Massachusetts.

1866 Susan B. Anthony, Lucy Stone, Elizabeth Cady Stanton, and Frederick Douglass organize the American Equal Rights Association (AERA).

1868 Susan B. Anthony, Elizabeth Cady Stanton, and Parker Pillsbury found a universal suffrage newspaper, the *Revolution.*

1869 Susan B. Anthony and Elizabeth Cady Stanton organize the National Woman Suffrage Association (NWSA); women are granted suffrage in the Wyoming Territory.

1870 Lucy Stone leaves the NWSA and forms the American Woman Suffrage Association (AWSA); the Fifteenth Amendment, granting suffrage to African American men, is ratified.

1872 Susan B. Anthony is arrested while attempting to vote in the presidential election.

1880 Lucretia Mott dies on November 11.

1885 Alice Paul is born in Mount Laurel, New Jersey, on January 11.

1890 The NWSA and AWSA unite to form the National American Woman Suffrage Association (NAWSA).

1893 Lucy Stone dies on October 18.

1902 Esther Morris dies on April 3; Elizabeth Cady Stanton dies on October 26.

1906 Susan B. Anthony dies on March 13.

1915 The women's suffrage amendment loses by a vote of 204 to 174 in the US House of Representatives.

1919 The US Senate passes the women's suffrage amendment by a vote of 56 to 25.

1920 The Nineteenth Amendment to the US Constitution is ratified, granting women the right to vote.

CHAPTER NOTES

CHAPTER 1
The Wyoming Experiment

1. T. A. Larson, *History of Wyoming*, 2nd edition (Lincoln, NE: University of Nebraska Press, 1978), p. 71.
2. Dorothy Gray, *Women of the West* (Lincoln, NE: University of Nebraska Press, 1998), p. 77.
3. Larson, p. 83.
4. Marcy Lynn Karin, "Esther Morris and Her Equality State: From Council Bill 70 to Life on the Bench," *American Journal of Legal History* 46, no. 3 (2004), p. 320.
5. Karin, p. 336.

CHAPTER 2
The United States: The Birthplace of Women's Suffrage

1. Marchette Chute, *The First Liberty: A History of the Right to Vote in America, 1619–1850* (New York, NY: Dutton, 1969), p. 196.
2. Elizabeth Cady Stanton, Susan B. Anthony, Matilda Joslyn Gage, and Ida Husted Harper, ed., *History of Woman Suffrage*, vol. 1 (New York, NY: Arno, 1969), p. 32.
3. Thomas Paine, *Common Sense* (New York, NY: Wiley, 1942), p. 53.
4. Olympe de Gouges, *The Declaration of the Rights of Woman* (September 1791), Liberty, Equality, Fraternity: Exploring the French Revolution, 2001, http://chnm.gmu.edu/revolution /d/477/.

CHAPTER 3
The Philosophy of Women's Suffrage

1. Mary Wollstonecraft, *A Vindication of the Rights of Woman*, Norton Critical Edition, ed. Carol H. Poston (New York, NY: Norton, 1988), p. 9.
2. Wollstonecraft, p. 12.
3. Wollstonecraft, p. 147.

4. Wollstonecraft, p. 242.
5. Martha J. Cutter, "Beyond Stereotypes: Mary Wilkins Freeman's Radical Critique of Nineteenth Century Cults of Femininity," *Women's Studies* 21 (1992), p. 384.
6. Cutter, p. 384.
7. De la Banta, *De la Banta's Advice to Ladies Concerning Beauty* (Chicago, IL: S. Junkin, 1878), p. 288, quoted in American Women: A Gateway to Library of Congress Resources for the Study of Women's History and Culture in the United States, http://memory.loc.gov/ammem/awhhtml/awgc1/etiquette .html (accessed March 18, 2008).
8. "Biographical Overview," Emma Willard School, http://www .emmawillard.org/about/history/ehwillard/ehwillard.php (accessed March 20, 2008).
9. Elisabeth Griffith, *In Her Own Right: The Life of Elizabeth Cady Stanton* (New York, NY: Oxford University Press, 1984), p. 18.
10. "Biographical Overview."
11. Sally Schwager, "Educating Women in America," *Signs* 12, no. 2 (1987), p. 343.

CHAPTER 4

Elizabeth Cady Stanton and the Seneca Falls Convention

1. Elizabeth Cady Stanton, *Elizabeth Cady Stanton as Revealed in Her Letters, Diary, and Reminiscences, vol. 1,* eds. Theodore Stanton and Harriot Stanton Blatch (New York, NY: Harper & Row, 1922), p. 79.
2. Frederick Douglass, "Why I Became a Woman's Rights Man," Audio Recording, Victory Audio Video Services, 1995.
3. Otelia Cromwell, *Lucretia Mott* (Cambridge, MA: Harvard University Press, 1958), p. 93.
4. Stanton, p. 145.
5. Elizabeth Cady Stanton, Susan B. Anthony, Matilda Joslyn Gage, and Ida Husted Harper, ed., *History of Woman Suffrage*, vol. 1 (New York, NY: Arno, 1969), p. 67.
6. Cady Stanton, Anthony, Gage, and Harper, p. 69.
7. Elisabeth Griffith, *In Her Own Right: The Life of Elizabeth Cady Stanton* (New York, NY: Oxford University Press, 1984), p. 57.

CHAPTER 5

Susan B. Anthony

1. Kathleen Barry, *Susan B. Anthony: A Biography of a Singular Feminist* (New York, NY: New York University Press, 1988), p. 23.
2. Barry, p. 25.
3. Elizabeth Cady Stanton, Susan B. Anthony, Matilda Joslyn Gage, and Ida Husted Harper, ed., *History of Woman Suffrage*, vol. 1 (New York, NY: Arno, 1969), p. 457.
4. Rosalyn Terborg-Penn, *African American Women in the Struggle for the Vote, 1850–1920* (Bloomington, IN: Indiana University Press, 1998).
5. Richard O. Reisem, "Rochester Remembers the Civil War with Cannon, Sculpture, and 399 Tombstones," *Epitaph Newsletter* 18, no. 2 (1998), http://www.lib.rochester.edu/index.cfm?PAGE=3098 (accessed June 25, 2007).

CHAPTER 6

The Fifteenth Amendment

1. Ida Husted Harper, *The Life and Work of Susan B. Anthony: Including Public Addresses, Her Own Letters and Many from Her Contemporaries During Fifty Years*, vol. 1 (New York, NY: Arno, 1969), p. 323.
2. Harper, p. 324.
3. Elizabeth Cady Stanton, Susan B. Anthony, Matilda Joslyn Gage, and Ida Husted Harper, ed., *History of Woman Suffrage*, vol. 2 (New York, NY: Arno, 1969), p. 757.
4. Greg Ross, "The Lucy Stone League," Futility Closet, October 5, 2017, https://www.futilitycloset.com/2017/10/05/lucy -stone-league/.
5. Kathleen Barry, *Susan B. Anthony: A Biography of a Singular Feminist* (New York, NY: New York University Press, 1988), p. 250.
6. *New York Times,* November 29, 1872, p. 1.
7. *The Times,* July 4, 1873, p. C5.

8. Rosalyn Terborg-Penn, *African American Women in the Struggle for the Vote, 1850–1920* (Bloomington, IN: Indiana University Press, 1998), p. 83.

CHAPTER 7

Victory

1. "Editorial," *Women's Studies* 1 (1973), p. 245.
2. Eleanor Flexner, *Century of Struggle: The Woman's Rights Movement in the United States* (Cambridge, MA: Belknap, 1959), p. 295.
3. Susan Goodier, *No Votes for Women: The New York State Anti-Suffrage Movement* (Chicago, IL: University of Illinois Press, 2013), p. 1.
4. Flexner, pp. 294–305.
5. Eileen L. McDonagh and H. Douglas Price, "Woman Suffrage in the Progressive Era: Patterns of Opposition and Support in Referenda Voting, 1910–1918," *American Political Science Review* 79, no. 2 (1985), p. 419.
6. Eleanor Clift, *Founding Sisters and the Nineteenth Amendment* (Hoboken, NJ: John Wiley & Sons, 2003), p. 91.
7. Flexner, p. 248
8. Clift, p. 91.
9. Clift, p. 92.
10. Flexner, p. 279.
11. Flexner, p. 282.

GLOSSARY

abolition The banning of slavery.

amendment A change to the US Constitution.

antisuffrage The belief that women should not have the right to vote.

ballot A piece of paper that casts a vote.

cult of domesticity The belief that women should not work outside the home.

enfranchisement The granting of the right to vote.

manumission Freedom from slavery.

militant Aggressive or combative.

misogyny The hatred of women.

Prohibition A ban on the sale of alcoholic drinks in the United States.

ratify To approve.

suffrage The right to vote.

suffragette A women's suffrage activist willing to break the law to gain suffrage.

suffragist A women's suffrage activist who believed in peaceful campaigning methods.

veto To deny.

FURTHER INFORMATION

BOOKS

Breen, Marta. *Fearless Females: The Fight for Freedom, Equality, and Sisterhood.* New York, NY: Yellow Jacket, 2019.

Cassidy, Tina. *Mr. President, How Long Must We Wait?: Alice Paul, Woodrow Wilson, and the Fight for the Right to Vote.* New York, NY: Atria, 2019.

Conkling, Winifred. *Votes for Women! American Suffragists and the Battle for the Ballot.* Chapel Hill, NC: Algonquin Young Readers, 2018.

Frazer, Coral Celeste. *Vote! Women's Fight for Access to the Ballot Box.* Minneapolis, MN: Twenty-First Century Books, 2019.

Kent, Deborah. *The Seneca Falls Convention: Working to Expand Women's Rights.* New York, NY: Enslow Publishing, 2017.

Wagner, Sally Roesch, ed. *The Women's Suffrage Movement.* New York, NY: Penguin, 2019.

Weiss, Elaine. *The Woman's Hour: The Great Fight to Win the Vote.* New York, NY: Viking, 2018.

WEBSITES

Library of Congress: Women's Suffrage
loc.gov/teachers/classroommaterials/primarysourcesets/womens-suffrage/
Check out a vast array of primary sources and visual materials.

National Archives: Woman Suffrage and the Nineteenth Amendment
www.archives.gov/education/lessons/woman-suffrage
View important documents related to the women's suffrage movement.

National Women's History Museum: Crusade for the Vote
www.crusadeforthevote.org
Explore the history of women's suffrage, a timeline, and links to primary resources.

FILMS

Not for Ourselves Alone: The Story of Elizabeth Cady Stanton and Susan B. Anthony (1999), directed by Ken Burns.

One Woman, One Vote (1995), directed by Ruth Pollack.

Suffragettes Forever! The Story of Women and Power (2018), directed by Jacqui Hayden.

INDEX